PERRY'S

DEPARTMENT STORE

DEPARTMENT STORE

A Buying Simulation for Juniors, Men's Wear,
Children's Wear, and Home Fashion/Giftware

3RD EDITION

Karen M. Videtic
VIRGINIA COMMONWEALTH UNIVERSITY

Cynthia W. Steele
C & F ENTERPRISES, INC.

FAIRCHILD BOOKS

NEW YORK

EXECUTIVE EDITOR: Olga T. Kontzias
SENIOR ASSOCIATE ACQUISITIONS EDITOR: Jaclyn Bergeron
SENIOR DEVELOPMENT EDITOR: Jennifer Crane
DEVELOPMENT EDITOR: Laurie Gibson
PRODUCTION DIRECTOR: Ginger Hillman
ASSOCIATE PRODUCTION EDITOR: Andrew Fargnoli
COPY EDITOR: Jeanne Ford
COVER DESIGN: StarGraphics Studio
COVER ART: iStockPhoto
Second Printing, 2010
Copyright © 2009 Fairchild Books, A Division of Condé Nast Publications, Inc.

LIBRARY OF CONGRESS CATALOG CARD NUMBER: 2008924430

ISBN: 978-1-56367-733-5

GST R 133004424

PRINTED IN THE UNITED STATES OF AMERICA

TP13

Contents

Extended Contents

Preface

Perry's Department Store: A Buying Simulation for Juniors, Men's Wear, Children's Wear, and Home Fashion/Giftware, 3rd Edition, attempts to bridge the gap between the principles of retail buying and mathematical formulas and concepts. It has been the authors' experience that students have difficulty with the application of mathematical models even though they are competent in the initial use of these formulas. This expanded text strengthens students' understanding of buyers' responsibilities by walking them through the various steps a new buyer would take to complete a six-month dollar plan and a merchandise assortment plan.

Two new chapters have been added to expand the practical information that a new buyer needs to know before going to market for the first time: Chapter 6, "How to Shop the Market," and Chapter 8, "Negotiating Profitability." These two chapters go beyond theory to explain the importance of preparation before the buyer enters the market; also discussed are methodology, shopping critically, cultural constraints, and ethical responsibilities of the buyer. Today's bottom-line organizations demand that a buyer maximize profits, including considerations such as a guaranteed gross margin. Negotiating is a learned skill and becomes even more difficult when the buyer must work across cultures. Several negotiating methods are reviewed in Chapter 8.

An accompanying CD-ROM now allows the student to follow the text's sequences and perform the corresponding steps and calculations more comfortably. This CD-ROM contains apparel and home fashion/giftware statistics plus material for buyers from actual buyers, manufacturers, and a trend analyst.

Perry's Department Store: A Buying Simulation is organized into 11 chapters. The book begins with background information about the fictitious Perry's, so students can become familiar with their new department and industry. As would any competent buyer, students must research new market and industry trends. When knowledgeable about their area, students proceed by projecting sales, beginning-of-the-month stock requirements, and markdowns to complete the six-month dollar plan.

It is not enough to project capital investment in merchandise. A buyer must be able to spend the dollar plan in the most effective and profitable way possible. The next step Perry's new buyer—the student—takes is to develop a merchandise assortment plan. This begins with the development of merchandise classifications and subclassifications, and culminates with an assortment plan detailing units purchased by price line, dollar, size, fabrication, and color.

No buyer's job would be complete without planning market trips and writing orders for actual merchandise. Although not all of the buyer's open-to-buy is spent, the simulation is almost complete when catalogues from prominent manufacturers are used to purchase merchandise for the department.

Today's department store buyer must find a niche to remain competitive with the numerous discounters and off-price merchandisers. Sales promotion has become one tool to help buyers effectively compete in the marketplace. Therefore, this simulation discusses the use of advertising, publicity, and public relations as they relate to an individual buyer's perspective, and examines their ability to increase sales of a department.

Although few buyers look beyond the gross margin of an income statement, the authors feel that students need to see the total financial picture to understand buyers' role in making a department profitable. The book therefore includes a chapter on profit and income statements as they relate to Perry's.

Product development has emerged as a vital method for buyers and their departments to remain competitive. Steps in the creation of a private label of merchandise for the target customer are discussed, along with the importance of fabric, sourcing, delivery, and technology.

Positions in retail buying—from assistant to general merchandise manager—are described in the final chapter. Included, too, are opportunities within buying groups.

The most significant feature of this text and CD-ROM is their ability to replicate real-life experience for students, so they can better understand the role of the retail buyer. The nature of simulation requires that students create an up-to-date business environment created as they research current market and industry trends. The text will not become dated because *students* continually provide the most current and contemporary information necessary to make their buying decisions.

Actual catalogues of nationally recognized manufacturers offer a realistic sampling of the real world as it relates to buying. The charts and forms in this book and CD-ROM are replicas of those found in the retail and wholesale industry and expose students to the procedures and policies they can expect to find in a first job as an assistant buyer or as a buying office clerk. Students may copy blank forms from the book or manipulate them electronically on the CD-ROM to use for worksheets and practice.

An instructor's guide is available to assist faculty with alternative viewpoints and opportunities for student discussion. This guide will also help the instructor who has never been a buyer and who may need additional information about resources, terminology, and other aspects unique to retail buying.

About the Authors

KAREN M. VIDETIC, chairperson and professor in the Department of Fashion Design and Merchandising at Virginia Commonwealth University (VCU), Richmond, Virginia, has taught retail buying, fashion, merchandising, advanced store development, management, and fashion promotions in VCU's Department of Fashion Design and Merchandising since 1984. Professor Videtic also taught fashion merchandising at J. Sargeant Reynolds Community College prior to teaching at VCU. Her bachelor's degree in marketing and distributive education, her masters of education in human resource development, and considerable course work toward a doctorate in urban services were all earned at VCU.

In 1997 Professor Videtic spent five months at the University of Ballarat outside of Melbourne, Australia, as a lecturer for the School of Business. She taught buyer behavior, contemporary issues in management, and human resource development on a graduate level, and also team-taught an undergraduate class in human resource development. She directed and led all international field trips to major fashion capitals such as Paris, London, Rome, Florence, and Hong Kong.

Professor Videtic's retail experience extends from department stores to national specialty chain stores, in both management and fashion promotion as well as independent consulting on merchandise planning and control. On the wholesale side of the fashion industry, Professor Videtic has assisted several independent manufacturers' sales representatives in both intimate apparel and fine jewelry, and attended New York and Atlanta markets. Her sales experience in the wholesale costume and fine jewelry industries is extensive; she has also developed numerous new product lines for national jewelry manufacturers.

Professor Videtic continues her consulting work, which includes merchandise planning for independent retailers and management seminars for AETA (American Equine Trade Association).

CYNTHIA W. STEELE is creative manager for C & F Enterprises, Inc., and Gallerie II, a leading wholesale company offering a complete line of bedding, home décor, and seasonal gifts. She is responsible for the trend and design direction for the company. Ms. Steele travels internationally to source product and work with factories.

Prior to this, she was vice president of product development for Evergreen Enterprises, Inc., a wholesale operation of flags, garden, and home décor products under the brands of Evergreen, Cypress Home, and Cape Craftsmen. Before joining Evergreen, Ms. Steele was a national account executive for New Creative Enterprises and Square Nest, a wholesaler of giftware and decorative accessories for the home and garden. She was responsible for national key account sales in the Northeast, planning domestic, custom, and import programs for buying organizations, department and chain stores, and catalogue operations.

Previously she was director of national accounts for Silvestri, a manufacturer of giftware, decorative accessories, collectible artist lines, and seasonal collections. As director, she was responsible for the key account sales of the company, overseeing the national accounts team. For buying offices, department stores, and chain stores, she developed both domestic and import programs.

Prior to joining Silvestri, Ms. Steele was operations manager for a local manufacturer's rep firm, overseeing the company sales representatives and serving as liaison with more than 30 vendors. In addition, she was responsible for handling key volume accounts for catalogue, military, chain stores, and a leading home shopping network. Her duties included managing sales, forecasting, and maintaining profit for a category in Wal-Mart's Retail Link™ Internet program. She has also coordinated programs and appeared as a guest host on QVC.

Formerly an assistant professor in the Department of Fashion at VCU, she has taught courses in apparel industry, retail buying, merchandising, trends, and fashion promotion.

Her professional background includes over 15 years' experience in retail buying and management for department, specialty, and independent stores. She has worked in children's wear, misses, junior, and women's sportswear, bridal and formalwear, men's wear, and fashion jewelry and accessories.

Ms. Steele earned a bachelor of fine arts degree in fashion design and a master's of education degree in adult education, specializing in human resource development. Both degrees are from VCU.

As a private consultant, Ms. Steele assists independent retailers with financial planning and merchandising.

Acknowledgments

The authors would like to acknowledge the following for their contributions to this edition:

LISA ARIOTTI, Fashion Sales and Production Assistant, Alpha Industries

DEIDRA ARRINGTON, Adjunct Professor, Virginia Commonwealth University

PATRICIA BREMAN, Senior Consultant, VALS Psychology of Markets

JENNIFER ERNST, Retail Coordinator, Jones New York

MICHAEL FISHER, Associate Fashion Director, Bloomingdale's

MICHELLE LAMB, Principal, Marketing Directions, Inc.

MICHELLE LANDON, Director of U.S. Fashion Sales, Alpha Industries

LISA MIRAVALLE, former department store buyer and divisional merchandising manager

SRI CONSULTING BUSINESS INTELLIGENCE

ROBERT VIDETIC, KBV Concepts

TING XU, President, Evergreen Enterprises Inc.

CHAPTER 1

INTRODUCTION

Perry's Background Information

IN THIS CHAPTER, YOU WILL LEARN:

* What a simulation is and how it is used
* The statistical and demographic information needed to make buying decisions
* How to analyze statistical information to define a customer base
* The breadth of a buyer's job and the function of the buyer within the retail organization

This chapter explains the simulation aspect of this textbook. It introduces a fictitious flagship store and its four branches. The location, sales volume, and customer profile is different for each branch store classification. Assuming the role of a newly promoted buyer, the student must research demographics and statistics, learn about market segmentation, and confront the responsibilities of a retail buyer. A step-by-step plan must be initiated before a market trip for the fall/holiday season.

OBJECTIVES OF THE SIMULATION

After completing the simulation in this book, students will be able to:

* Understand how and why buying decisions are made, as demonstrated through this buying simulation

* Understand the breadth of the buyer's role in a retail organization

* Research market trends and industry trends

* Apply buying formulas and mathematical examples in a realistic format

* Plan model stock for a department within a retail organization

* Understand how market segmentation is used in a retail setting

* Understand the role of the buyer in the product development process

* Recognize the changing responsibilities of the buyer today

THE SIMULATION: WHAT IS IT AND HOW DOES IT WORK?

A simulation can be defined as a similar situation, resembling but not exactly like the conditions that exist in reality. For the sake of this simulation, you will be provided with the statistical and demographic information necessary to make buying decisions. It will be your responsibility to supply the logic and the supplemental materials to substantiate your merchandising decisions.

Perry's is fictitious, as is the statistical information, and is in no way representative of a specific retail organization.

PERRY'S DEMOGRAPHIC INFORMATION

Perry's is a small, suburban department store located in Fredericksburg, Virginia. The flagship store is located downtown, with four branch operations in local shopping malls within a 40-mile radius of downtown.

Fredericksburg is located approximately 45 miles south of Washington, DC, and 45 miles north of Richmond, Virginia. It is fast becoming a suburb of the Washington area, and a commuter train currently connects Union Station in Washington with downtown Fredericksburg.

As is much of Virginia, Fredericksburg is important in Southern history, and it offers several historical tourist attractions. It is also the home of Mary Washington College, a four-year liberal arts institution.

The city of Fredericksburg is surrounded by three counties: Caroline, Spotsylvania, and Stafford. Stafford and Spotsylvania are two of the fastest-growing counties in Virginia and rank in the top 100 fastest-growing counties in the United States. Caroline is a relatively rural community. (Figure 1.1 is a *Women's Wear Daily* article discussing WorldStreet and Celebrate Virginia, a significant addition to the retail landscape surrounding the Fredericksburg region.)

Mignatti Envisions a Brave New "World"

Evan Clark

FREDERICKSBURG, VA—After a helicopter tour of the future home of WorldStreet, a retail concept that will be part mall, part bow to the forces of globalization, a group of Venezuelan investors emptied their water bottles so they could take dirt home from the construction site.

"How great is that? That's an investment in the American dream," said David Mignatti, who is spearheading the project as president of the WorldStreet Development Division of Silver Cos., the master developer.

Now just a patch of barren ground within the confines of Celebrate Virginia, a massive retail complex created by Silver Cos., WorldStreet is set to open in 2008 and aims to be a new story line in the tale of globalization, one that will diminish the roles of major retailers and instead offer an outlet to relatively nameless manufacturers.

Celebrate Virginia spans 2,400 acres along Interstate 95 between Washington and Richmond. Billed as "North America's Largest Retail Resort," it will be home to historic attractions such as the National Slavery Museum (opening next year) and Central Park, a 2.4 million-square-foot mixed-use retail and entertainment complex featuring restaurants and stores ranging from Wal-Mart to Talbot's, an indoor ice skating rink, a convention center and an indoor water park.

The $200 million-plus WorldStreet project will be a quarter of a mile long, house 250 to 300 stores, six eateries and a dozen or more cafes over 750,000 square feet. The roster is still being worked out, but Mignatti expects about half the stores at WorldStreet to be operated by foreign companies, some of which produce goods for well-known retailers but haven't had their own storefront in the U.S.

Among those confirmed to be taking space at WorldStreet are Far East Imports, based in Alexandria, Va., which specializes in hand-painted vases from China and the Far East, accessories company Mediterranean Treasures and a jewelry firm from Jaipur, India.

"WorldStreet represents an opportunity to take links out of the supply chain," said Mignatti, who recounted the story about the Venezuelans during a recent tour of the site.

"Victoria's Secret wouldn't be a chain store that would be in WorldStreet, but perhaps one of the manufacturers and exporters that sell lingerie to Victoria's Secret would establish their own brand at WorldStreet," said Mignatti. "The industry is changing worldwide, manufacturers are looking for future solutions, and one of the solutions is going direct to the consumer."

Given the dramatic growth among discounters, continued expansion of single-brand specialty stores and consolidation among department stores, at least some overseas manufacturers need a new outlet.

"It's not easy these days for manufacturers to get ahead," said retail consultant Walter Loeb, who was not familiar with WorldStreet but said the project could be an opportunity for some firms. "Those manufacturers who are anchored to Federated or somebody are not likely to go that route because they're afraid of losing that contact, that customer. If you're not one of the strong first-line resources used by the retailers . . . you're trying to find other ways to get contact with the customer, support the customer and then the growth through that demand."

To find prospective firms, WorldStreet is reaching out around the world.

Mignatti recently spent two weeks promoting the project in China and has 27 private companies from that country scheduled to visit the site by mid-February. Slots have already been sold to firms from China, India, Turkey, Venezuela and Ecuador, and apparel is expected to make up about 30 percent to 35 percent of the project.

In a departure from the normal mall format, companies will own their stores under a commercial condominium arrangement, and 75 percent of the purchase can be financed by Silver Cos.

The idea is to bring in new players with goods that have the ability to create a brand identity and then help them expand through print, Web, TV and radio ads and business support services from access to logistic services to store design advice and merchant banking.

"We're selling opportunity. This isn't just another real estate development project," Mignatti said. "We're inviting new participants."

In addition to foreign firms, WorldStreet is courting U.S. brands that don't have the ubiquity of well-developed national names and boutique owners looking to expand. A branded presence to draw consumers might be key to the endeavor.

"WorldStreet's going to need anchors of brands to attract people," said Andrew Jassin, managing director of the Jassin-O'Rourke Group, a fashion consultancy. "Without that, I think it's a challenge in today's climate."

Mignatti said stores at WorldStreet will also act as wholesale showrooms, where brands can establish a distribution beachhead in the U.S. and haggle with store buyers. Brands can also buy space at the center's warehouse distribution facilities to service wholesale clients.

This mixture of wholesale and retail, as well as the ability of the brands to own their stores, is in line with the way business is conducted outside the U.S., said Larry Silver, chief executive officer of Silver Cos., who has led the company since 1972.

In addition to bringing a bit of a foreign operating ethos to the U.S., the cen-

FIGURE 1.1   Demographic profile of Fredericksburg, VA

continued

ter is intended to deliver an international feel to Virginia.

"We're bringing an opportunity to experience a new lifestyle to the American public that, unless they got to travel to the bazaars of the world, they would never get to experience," said Silver.

WorldStreet, as he tells it, will be awash in the smells of exotic cuisines and the sounds of foreign languages. "The owners and merchants themselves will be working in these facilities," said Silver.

The project also helps Silver get around a problem as a retail developer.

"Our industry is starving for new anchors," he said, noting there are only so many Targets and Wal-Marts and Lowe's to build around.

A Wal-Mart superstore weighs in at about 250,000 square feet, while WorldStreets—there are plans to develop about a dozen more near major U.S. cities—could top 1 million square feet. "That is a tremendous anchor," said Silver. "We become the center of a gigantic draw, a phenomenal experience."

The center, like Celebrate Virginia, is designed to create a critical mass of shopping to draw people from farther away and to get them to spend more. WorldStreet will connect with other attractions at Celebrate Virginia—the entertainment district, the convention center and hotels—by buses and rubber-tire trolleys. These will convey shoppers along some of Celebrate Virginia's more than seven miles of internal six-lane parkways, some of which now lead through empty fields being prepared for construction.

Already there is a seemingly endless collection of stores. There is one point where shoppers could see at least four stores offering $5,000 flat-screen TVs and drive no more than 30 seconds between them, amounting to what Mignatti said is an important component of the project: the "comparative shopping experience."

Still, the striving for critical mass that is a hallmark of the project begs the question: How much retail can the market bear?

For Mignatti, the field is wide open.

"America's great pastime is consumerism—more than sports, more than arts, more than culture," he said. "We are a country of consumers and shoppers. These projects respond to the demands."

FIGURE 1.1 (CONTINUED)

The following tables include some statistics for the city of Fredericksburg and the three surrounding counties. Use Spotsylvania's demographics for Dale City.

TABLE 1.1

DEMOGRAPHIC PROFILE OF FREDERICKSBURG, VA					
	2000 CENSUS			**2006 ESTIMATES**	
Total Population:	19,279			21,273	
GENDER:					
Male	8,677	45.0		9,634	45.3%
Female	10,602	55.0		11,639	54.7%
AGE:					
Under 5 years	1,127	5.8%	Under 5 years	1,997	9.39%
5 to 9	943	4.9%	5 to 9	1,045	4.91%
10 to 14	867	4.5%	10 to 14	958	4.50%
15 to 19	2,104	10.9%	15 to 19	2,362	11.10%
20 to 24	2,982	15.5%	20 to 24	3,349	15.74%
25 to 34	2,856	14.8%	25 to 34	3,248	15.27%
35 to 44	2,385	12.4%	35 to 44	2,496	11.73%
45 to 54	2,138	11.1%	45 to 54	2,103	9.89%
55 to 59	791	4.1%	55 to 59	955	4.49%
60 to 64	616	3.2%	60 to 64	796	3.74%
65 to 74	1,222	6.3%	65 to 74	1,091	5.13%
75 to 84	926	4.8%	75 to 84	943	4.43%
85 and over	322	1.7%	85 and over	309	1.45%
Median Age		30.3			30.2
High School Graduate and Above		80.2%			80.2%
Median Household Income		$34,585			$41,488
Median Family Income		$47,148			N/A
Total Housing Units		8,888			9,618

continued

TABLE I.I (CONTINUED)

POPULATION BY RACE/ETHNICITY FOR FREDERICKSBURG, VA

	2000 CENSUS		2006 ESTIMATES	
Total Population:	19,279		21,273	
RACE:				
White	14,108	73.2%	15,940	74.9%
Black or African American	3,935	20.4%	4,373	20.6%
American Indian or Alaska Native	65	0.3%	75	0.4%
Asian	291	1.5%	391	1.8%
Native Hawaiian/Pacific Islander	11	0.1%	13	0.1%
Other and Multi-Race	869	4.5%	481	2.3%
ETHNICITY:				
Hispanic or Latino	945	4.9%	1,572	7.4%

SOURCE: U.S. Census Bureau, 2000 Census, 2006 American Community Survey.

TABLE I.2

POPULATION PROJECTIONS BY GENDER AND AGE FOR FREDERICKSBURG, VA

	2010 PROJECTIONS		2020 PROJECTIONS		2030 PROJECTIONS	
Total Population:	22,239		25,116		28,518	
GENDER:						
Male	9,928	44.6%	11,293	45.0%	12,538	44.0%
Female	12,311	55.4%	13,823	55.0%	15,980	56.0%
AGE:						
Under 5 years	1,670	7.5%	1,889	8.5%	2,028	9.1%
5 to 9	1,018	4.6%	1,217	5.5%	1,338	6.0%
10 to 14	790	3.6%	905	4.1%	1,054	4.7%
15 to 19	2,202	9.9%	2,053	9.2%	2,379	10.7%

continued

TABLE 1.2 (CONTINUED)

POPULATION PROJECTIONS BY GENDER AND AGE FOR FREDERICKSBURG, VA

AGE:	2010 PROJECTIONS		2020 PROJECTIONS		2030 PROJECTIONS	
20 to 24	2,956	13.3%	2,668	12.0%	3,014	13.6%
25 to 29	2,129	9.6%	2,397	10.8%	2,282	10.3%
30 to 34	1,554	7.0%	1,889	8.5%	1,756	7.9%
35 to 39	1,126	5.1%	1,383	6.2%	1,602	7.2%
40 to 44	1,014	4.6%	1,143	5.1%	1,381	6.2%
45 to 49	1,199	5.4%	1,097	4.9%	1,349	6.1%
50 to 54	1,232	5.5%	1,196	5.4%	1,341	6.0%
55 to 59	1,135	5.1%	1,346	6.1%	1,240	5.6%
60 to 64	975	4.4%	1,223	5.5%	1,177	5.3%
65 to 69	799	3.6%	1,231	5.5%	1,439	6.5%
70 to 74	697	3.1%	1,223	5.5%	1,526	6.9%
75 to 79	626	2.8%	849	3.8%	1,308	5.9%
80 to 84	497	2.2%	566	2.5%	1,030	4.6%
85 and over	620	2.8%	841	3.8%	1,274	5.7%

POPULATION PROJECTIONS BY RACE/ETHNICITY FOR FREDERICKSBURG, VA

	2010 PROJECTIONS		2020 PROJECTIONS		2030 PROJECTIONS	
Total Population:	22,239		25,116		28,518	
RACE:						
White	15,777	70.9%	7,257	28.9%	18,873	66.2%
Black or African American	4,642	20.9%	5,619	22.4%	6,870	24.1%
American Indian or Alaska Native	66	0.3%	72	0.3%	56	0.2%
Asian	365	1.6%	453	1.8%	575	2.0%
ETHNICITY:						
Hispanic or Latino	1,389	6.2%	1,715	6.8%	2,144	7.5%

SOURCE: U.S. Census Bureau, Virginia Employment Commission.

TABLE 1.3

DEMOGRAPHIC PROFILE OF CAROLINE COUNTY, VA					
	2000 CENSUS			**2006 ESTIMATES**	
Total Population:	22,121			26,731	
GENDER:					
Male	11,011	49.8%		13,303	49.8%
Female	11,110	50.2%		13,428	50.2%
AGE:					
Under 5 years	1,381	6.2%	Under 5 years	1,606	6.01%
5 to 9	1,559	7.0%	5 to 9	1,758	6.58%
10 to 14	1,602	7.2%	10 to 14	1,722	6.44%
15 to 19	1,424	6.4%	15 to 19	1,662	6.22%
20 to 24	1,153	5.2%	20 to 24	1,381	5.17%
25 to 34	2,915	13.2%	25 to 34	3,029	11.33%
35 to 44	3,696	16.7%	35 to 44	3,846	14.39%
45 to 54	3,188	14.4%	45 to 54	3,933	14.71%
55 to 59	1,318	6.0%	55 to 59	1,924	7.20%
60 to 64	1,028	4.6%	60 to 64	1,402	5.24%
65 to 74	1,569	7.1%	65 to 74	1,943	7.27%
75 to 84	960	4.3%	75 to 84	1,281	4.79%
85 and over	328	1.5%	85 and over	318	1.19%
Median Age		37.70			36.20
High School Graduate and Above		71.30%			N/A
Median Household Income		$39,845			$44,212
Median Family Income		$43,533			N/A
Total Housing Units		8,889			10,369

continued

TABLE I.3 (CONTINUED)

POPULATION BY RACE/ETHNICITY FOR CAROLINE COUNTY, VA

	2000 CENSUS		2006 ESTIMATES	
Total Population:	22,121		26,731	
RACE:				
White	13,842	62.6%	18,140	67.9%
Black or African American	7,604	34.4%	7,800	29.2%
American Indian or Alaska Native	172	0.8%	202	0.8%
Asian	79	0.4%	213	0.8%
Native Hawaiian/Pacific Islander	6	0.0%	5	0.0%
Other and Multi-Race	418	1.9%	371	1.4%
ETHNICITY:				
Hispanic or Latino	295	1.3%	810	3.0%

SOURCE: U.S. Census Bureau, 2000 Census, 2006 American Community Survey.

TABLE I.4

POPULATION PROJECTIONS BY AGE AND GENDER FOR CAROLINE COUNTY, VA

	2010 PROJECTIONS		2020 PROJECTIONS		2030 PROJECTIONS	
Total Population:	29,201		36,058		43,662	
GENDER:						
Male	14,468	49.5%	17,812	49.4%	21,394	49.0%
Female	14,733	50.5%	18,246	50.6%	22,268	51.0%
AGE:						
Under 5 years	1,864	6.4%	2,375	8.1%	2,872	9.8%
5 to 9	1,769	6.1%	2,324	8.0%	2,893	9.9%
10 to 14	1,662	5.7%	2,192	7.5%	2,767	9.5%
15 to 19	1,774	6.1%	1,906	6.5%	2,497	8.6%

continued

TABLE 1.4 (CONTINUED)

POPULATION PROJECTIONS BY AGE AND GENDER FOR CAROLINE COUNTY, VA

AGE:	2010 PROJECTIONS		2020 PROJECTIONS		2030 PROJECTIONS	
20 to 24	1,978	6.8%	1,942	6.7%	2,529	8.7%
25 to 29	2,350	8.0%	2,554	8.7%	2,693	9.2%
30 to 34	1,944	6.7%	2,680	9.2%	2,601	8.9%
35 to 39	1,729	5.9%	2,781	9.5%	2,956	10.1%
40 to 44	2,027	6.9%	2,339	8.0%	3,142	10.8%
45 to 49	2,365	8.1%	2,106	7.2%	3,265	11.2%
50 to 54	2,208	7.6%	2,408	8.2%	2,738	9.4%
55 to 59	1,828	6.3%	2,657	9.1%	2,358	8.1%
60 to 64	1,731	5.9%	2,306	7.9%	2,534	8.7%
65 to 69	1,271	4.4%	1,725	5.9%	2,513	8.6%
70 to 74	934	3.2%	1,451	5.0%	1,942	6.7%
75 to 79	712	2.4%	980	3.4%	1,332	4.6%
80 to 84	543	1.9%	639	2.2%	993	3.4%
85 and over	512	1.8%	693	2.4%	1,037	3.6%

POPULATION PROJECTIONS BY RACE/ETHNICITY FOR CAROLINE COUNTY, VA

	2010 PROJECTIONS		2020 PROJECTIONS		2030 PROJECTIONS	
Total Population:	29,201		36,058		43,662	
RACE:						
White	19,014	65.1%	23,528	65.3%	28,131	64.4%
Black or African American	9,213	31.6%	11,035	30.6%	13,154	30.1%
American Indian or Alaska Native	229	0.8%	304	0.8%	391	0.9%
Asian	157	0.5%	271	0.8%	525	1.2%
ETHNICITY:						
Hispanic or Latino	588	2.0%	920	2.6%	1,461	3.3%

SOURCE: U.S. Census Bureau, Virginia Employment Commission

TABLE 1.5

DEMOGRAPHIC PROFILE OF SPOTSYLVANIA COUNTY, VA

	2000 CENSUS		2006 ESTIMATES	
Total Population:	90,395		119,529	
GENDER:				
Male	44,532	49.3%	57,985	48.5%
Female	45,863	50.7%	61,544	51.5%
AGE:				
Under 5 years	6,879	7.6%	Under 5 years	8,604	7.20%
5 to 9	7,894	8.7%	5 to 9	7,656	6.41%
10 to 14	8,008	8.9%	10 to 14	9,466	7.92%
15 to 19	6,350	7.0%	15 to 19	9,034	7.56%
20 to 24	4,603	5.1%	20 to 24	8,221	6.88%
25 to 34	12,552	13.9%	25 to 34	18,327	15.33%
35 to 44	16,510	18.3%	35 to 44	19,731	16.51%
45 to 54	12,846	14.2%	45 to 54	17,873	14.95%
55 to 59	4,184	4.6%	55 to 59	6,700	5.61%
60 to 64	3,043	3.4%	60 to 64	4,170	3.49%
65 to 74	4,342	4.8%	65 to 74	5,313	4.44%
75 to 84	2,443	2.7%	75 to 84	3,467	2.90%
85 and over	741	0.8%	85 and over	967	0.81%
Median Age		34.3			30.2
High School Graduate and Above		83.8%			89.1%
Median Household Income		$57,525			$72,453
Median Family Income		$62,422			$75,507
Total Housing Units		33,329			43,544

continued

TABLE I.5 (CONTINUED)

POPULATION BY RACE/ETHNICITY FOR SPOTSYLVANIA COUNTY, VA

	2000 CENSUS		2006 ESTIMATES	
Total Population:	90,395		119,529	
RACE:				
White	74,924	82.9%	93,535	78.3%
Black or African American	11,255	12.5%	17,264	14.4%
American Indian or Alaska Native	288	0.3%	180	0.2%
Asian	1,243	1.4%	2,388	2.0%
Native Hawaiin/Pacific Islander	45	0.0%	156	0.1%
Other and Multi-Race	2,640	2.9%	6,006	5.0%
ETHNICITY:				
Hispanic or Latino	2,536	2.8%	7,152	6.0%

SOURCE: U.S. Census Bureau, 2000 Census, 2006 American Community Survey.

TABLE I.6

POPULATION PROJECTIONS BY AGE AND GENDER FOR SPOTSYLVANIA COUNTY, VA

	2010 PROJECTIONS		2020 PROJECTIONS		2030 PROJECTIONS	
Total Population:	134,163		175,402		217,797	
GENDER:						
Male	66,471	49.5%	86,881	49.5%	107,606	49.4%
Female	67,692	50.5%	88,521	50.5%	110,191	50.6%
AGE:						
Under 5 years	9,430	7.0%	12,483	9.3%	14,748	11.0%
5 to 9	9,628	7.2%	13,008	9.7%	15,671	11.7%
10 to 14	9,379	7.0%	12,163	9.1%	15,601	11.6%
15 to 19	9,799	7.3%	10,892	8.1%	14,383	10.7%

continued

TABLE 1.6 (CONTINUED)

POPULATION PROJECTIONS BY AGE AND GENDER FOR SPOTSYLVANIA COUNTY, VA

	2010 PROJECTIONS		2020 PROJECTIONS		2030 PROJECTIONS	
AGE:						
20 to 24	10,571	7.9%	11,247	8.4%	14,144	10.5%
25 to 29	10,252	7.6%	13,507	10.1%	14,350	10.7%
30 to 34	10,080	7.5%	14,456	10.8%	14,896	11.1%
35 to 39	9,322	6.9%	13,138	9.8%	16,816	12.5%
40 to 44	9,685	7.2%	12,136	9.0%	16,763	12.5%
45 to 49	10,068	7.5%	10,413	7.8%	14,153	10.5%
50 to 54	9,324	6.9%	10,231	7.6%	12,605	9.4%
55 to 59	7,883	5.9%	10,651	7.9%	10,887	8.1%
60 to 64	6,783	5.1%	9,872	7.4%	10,541	7.9%
65 to 69	4,136	3.1%	7,472	5.6%	9,826	7.3%
70 to 74	2,891	2.2%	6,063	4.5%	8,566	6.4%
75 to 79	1,996	1.5%	3,306	2.5%	5,828	4.3%
80 to 84	1,387	1.0%	1,936	1.4%	3,948	2.9%
85 and over	1,549	1.2%	2,428	1.8%	4,071	3.0%

POPULATION PROJECTIONS BY RACE/ETHNICITY FOR SPOTSYLVANIA COUNTY, VA

	2010 PROJECTIONS		2020 PROJECTIONS		2030 PROJECTIONS	
Total Population:	134,163		175,402		217,797	
RACE:						
White	105,442	78.6%	133,780	76.3%	159,361	73.2%
Black or African American	19,491	14.5%	27,513	15.7%	38,000	17.4%
American Indian or Alaska Native	355	0.3%	384	0.2%	390	0.2%
Asian	2,764	2.1%	4,346	2.5%	6,439	3.0%
ETHNICITY:						
Hispanic or Latino	6,111	4.6%	9,379	5.3%	13,607	6.2%

SOURCE: U.S. Census Bureau, Virginia Employment Commission·

TABLE 1.7

DEMOGRAPHIC PROFILE OF STAFFORD COUNTY, VA					
	2000 CENSUS			**2006 ESTIMATES**	
Total Population:	22,121			26,731	
GENDER:					
Male	11,011	49.8%		13,303	49.8%
Female	11,110	50.2%		13,428	50.2%
AGE:					
Under 5 years	7,172	7.8%	Under 5 years	8,216	6.84%
5 to 9	8,559	9.3%	5 to 9	7,542	6.28%
10 to 14	8,632	9.3%	10 to 14	10,901	9.07%
15 to 19	6,974	7.5%	15 to 19	10,413	8.67%
20 to 24	5,027	5.4%	20 to 24	9,054	7.53%
25 to 34	12,853	13.9%	25 to 34	16,811	13.99%
35 to 44	18,272	19.8%	35 to 44	20,583	17.13%
45 to 54	12,958	14.0%	45 to 54	18,647	15.52%
55 to 59	4,067	4.4%	55 to 59	6,714	5.59%
60 to 64	2,458	2.7%	60 to 64	4,514	3.76%
65 to 74	3,256	3.5%	65 to 74	4,064	3.38%
75 to 84	1,670	1.8%	75 to 84	2,146	1.79%
85 and over	548	0.6%	85 and over	565	0.47%
Median Age		33.1			33.6
High School Graduate and Above		80.9%			91.4%
Median Household Income		$59,618			$85,014
Median Family Income		$89,300			$93,625
Total Housing Units		20,529			41,791

continued

TABLE I.7 (CONTINUED)

POPULATION BY RACE/ETHNICITY FOR STAFFORD COUNTY, VA

	2000 CENSUS		2006 ESTIMATES	
Total Population:	92,446		120,170	
RACE:				
White	75,807	82.0%	88,419	73.6%
Black or African American	1,121	1.2%	20,283	16.9%
American Indian or Alaska Native	417	0.5%	103	0.1%
Asian	1,512	1.6%	2,991	2.5%
Native Hawaiian/Pacific Islander	93	0.1%	323	0.3%
Other and Multi-Race	3,406	3.7%	8,051	6.7%
ETHNICITY:				
Hispanic or Latino	3,342	3.6%	9,103	7.6%

SOURCE: U.S. Census Bureau, 2000 Census, 2006 American Community Survey.

TABLE I.8

POPULATION PROJECTIONS BY GENDER AND AGE FOR STAFFORD COUNTY, VA

	2010 PROJECTIONS		2020 PROJECTIONS		2030 PROJECTIONS	
Total Population:	135,806		176,710		218,772	
GENDER:						
Male	68,430	50.4%	88,748	50.2%	109,548	50.1%
Female	67,376	49.6%	87,962	49.8%	109,224	49.9%
AGE:						
Under 5 years	9,222	6.8%	12,093	8.9%	14,246	10.5%
5 to 9	9,017	6.6%	11,906	8.8%	14,646	10.8%
10 to 14	9,392	6.9%	11,129	8.2%	14,302	10.5%
15 to 19	10,314	7.6%	9,910	7.3%	12,904	9.5%

continued

TABLE 1.8 (CONTINUED)

POPULATION PROJECTIONS BY GENDER AND AGE FOR STAFFORD COUNTY, VA

	2010 PROJECTIONS		2020 PROJECTIONS		2030 PROJECTIONS	
AGE:						
20 to 24	11,880	8.7%	11,828	8.7%	13,670	10.1%
25 to 29	12,070	8.9%	15,163	11.2%	14,111	10.4%
30 to 34	9,519	7.0%	15,649	11.5%	15,063	11.1%
35 to 39	8,713	6.4%	14,541	10.7%	17,969	13.2%
40 to 44	9,890	7.3%	11,293	8.3%	17,981	13.2%
45 to 49	11,565	8.5%	10,122	7.5%	16,313	12.0%
50 to 54	10,184	7.5%	11,012	8.1%	12,489	9.2%
55 to 59	8,003	5.9%	12,316	9.1%	10,893	8.0%
60 to 64	6,298	4.6%	10,468	7.7%	11,364	8.4%
65 to 69	4,068	3.0%	7,701	5.7%	11,781	8.7%
70 to 74	2,165	1.6%	5,322	3.9%	8,836	6.5%
75 to 79	1,493	1.1%	3,305	2.4%	6,230	4.6%
80 to 84	1,065	0.8%	1,572	1.2%	3,779	2.8%
85 and over	948	0.7%	1,380	1.0%	2,195	1.6%

POPULATION PROJECTIONS BY RACE/ETHNICITY FOR STAFFORD COUNTY, VA

	2010 PROJECTIONS		2020 PROJECTIONS		2030 PROJECTIONS	
Total Population:	135,806		176,710		218,772	
RACE:						
White	102,802	75.7%	130,670	73.9%	156,792	71.7%
Black or African American	21,050	15.5%	27,798	15.7%	35,140	16.1%
American Indian or Alaska Native	706	0.5%	855	0.5%	957	0.4%
Asian	3,620	2.7%	5,849	3.3%	9,074	4.1%
ETHNICITY:						
Hispanic or Latino	7,628	5.6%	11,538	6.5%	16,809	7.7%

SOURCE: U.S. Census Bureau, Virginia Employment Commission ·

TABLE 1.9

RETAIL SALES HISTORY		
LOCALITY	**ESTABLISHMENTS**	**TOTAL RETAIL SALES**
Spotsylvania	267	$1,170,499,000
Fredericksburg	350	$795,191,000
Stafford	221	$614,479,000
Caroline	72	$256,890,000

SOURCE: U.S. Census Bureau, 2002 American Community Survey.

PERRY'S STATISTICAL INFORMATION

Perry's classifies its branch stores by a ranking of A, B, or C, according to sales volume and the progressive styling of the consumer who patronizes each branch. Many department stores rank their branch stores this way, using an alphabetical ranking system—A, B, C, D, E, etc.; others may use similar methods. Some of the reasons stores are ranked in this manner are to plan:

1. Square footage

2. Interior decor

3. Fixtures

4. Sales volume

5. Inventory levels

6. Stock assortment

7. Store personnel

8. Consumer profile

A stores have the highest sales volume and usually receive an additional layer of upscale, fashion merchandise. Typically, A stores have a higher average purchase than B or C stores.

B stores have the next highest sales volume and inventory levels. C stores are average, with a lesser sales volume than A and B stores and an inventory that reflects the taste level of the average consumer, the largest portion of the population.

At Perry's, A stores generate a sales volume close to or above $14 million and cater to an upper- to middle-income consumer with classic to progressive taste who probably commutes north to the metropolitan Washington area. These consumers are white-collar professionals working in an office environment.

Perry's B stores produce a sales volume between $12 million and $13 million, obtained from conservative, middle-income families with members who probably work within a 15- to 20-mile radius of the store. Style and value are of equal importance.

Perry's has one C store with a lower sales volume, under $5 million, which is patronized by a consumer who places value before style. A C store consumer is probably a "local" or longtime resident of the Fredericksburg area and may well live in a rural area.

Table 1.10 shows how Perry's rates its stores according to the sales volume and the progressive styling of the consumer who patronizes each branch.

TABLE 1.10

TOTAL YEARLY SALES BY STORE			
STORE CLASSIFICATION	LOCATION	SALES VOLUME	PERCENT OF TOTAL
A Store	Spotsylvania	$15,575,000	26.0
A Store	Fredericksburg	$14,000,000	23.3
B Store	Dale City	$12,900,000	21.5
B Store	Stafford	$12,750,000	21.3
C Store	Caroline	$ 4,775,000	7.9
TOTAL		$60,000,000	100.0

PERRY'S: A TRADITIONAL ORGANIZATION

As you will see in Figure 1.2, Perry's is organized as a traditional department store, with five functions.

The merchandise function involves the purchasing of merchandise for retail sale. The vice president of merchandising oversees general merchandise managers (GMMs), divisional merchandise managers (DMMs), buyers, and assistant buyers. The vice president of operations is responsible for handling all aspects of the retail stores. Reporting to the vice president of operations are the warehouse and store managers, department sales managers, and salespeople. The vice president of sales promotion is in charge of advertising, public relations, and visual merchandising. Accounts payable/receivable, inventory control, customer charge accounts, merchandise information systems, and finance are controlled by the vice president of finance. The vice president of human resources is responsible for the hiring, maintaining, and training of store personnel. Buyers at Perry's, as with any department store, must interact with all functions to maximize the potential and profit of their department.

Buying and selling functions are separated at Perry's. This means that buyers do not directly supervise the sales staff. However, because of the proximity of the stores, buyers are significantly involved with sales training and merchandise layout for the departmental sales floor.

The responsibilities of a buyer employed by Perry's include:

1. Development of a six-month dollar buying plan for all five stores

2. Development of model stock plans by classification, subclassification, price line, color, units, size, and fabrication for all five stores

3. Trend analysis (in report form)
   a. Use of buying office as a main source of trend information

4. Vendor analysis (in report form)
   a. Sales performance
   b. Markdown allowance (dollars and percentages)

5. Education of sales personnel, to include:
   a. Merchandising of new trends
   b. Front- and forward-featured merchandise schedule
   c. Sales promotions and special events

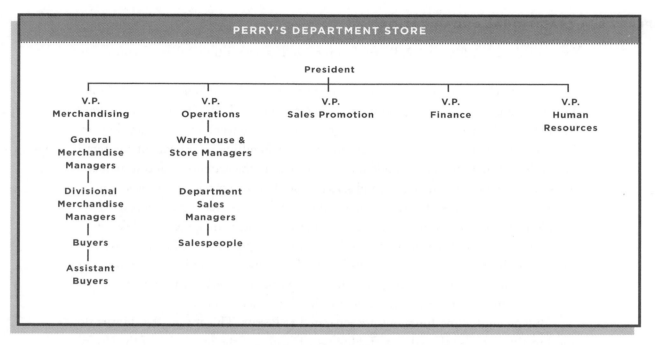

FIGURE 1.2   Organization chart for Perry's Department Store

6. Supervision of assistant buyers or other buying office staff

7. Development of long-range departmental goals

8. Selection of merchandise at market according to approved plans

9. Accurate recording of all purchases, transfers, and returns to vendors that affect the value of departmental inventory

10. Promotional plans for department, to include:
   a. Signing of merchandise
   b. Cooperative advertising assistance (vendor and dollars)
   c. Merchandise to be promoted

11. Communication with department's sales manager, to include:
   a. Sales goals (daily/monthly)
   b. Shortage goals
   c. Special promotions (advertising, fashion shows, etc.)
   d. Markdowns and transfer requests

12. Communication with divisional merchandise manager and general merchandise managers, to include:
    a. Accurate and timely stock plans
    b. Presentation of orders for approval
    c. Sales data
    d. Updates on open-to-buy

You have been with Perry's as an assistant buyer since graduation from college four years ago. A buying position has opened and you have been offered the job. You have been given 60 days to reorganize and develop a step-by-step plan before your first market trip to purchase the fall/holiday season. For the purpose of this simulation, you will need to select one of the following departments: Children's Wear, Juniors, Men's Wear, or Home Fashion/Giftware.

Your step-by-step plan is as follows:

STEP ONE	Redefine Perry's customer for your area
STEP TWO	Research and report on current fashion and industry trends
STEP THREE	Develop the fall/holiday six-month buying plan
STEP FOUR	Develop stock assortment plans
STEP FIVE	Plan market purchases
STEP SIX	Examine the income statement

There are guidelines for each step of your plan. Remember to justify all of your conclusions, as you are being scrutinized by upper management.

CHAPTER 2

STEP ONE

Redefine Your Customer

IN THIS CHAPTER, YOU WILL LEARN:

* How to apply statistical information to develop a customer profile for A, B, and C stores
* What publications are used in various segments of the fashion industry

Your first assignment as a new buyer is to redefine Perry's customer for your department. Use the demographic and statistical information offered in Chapter 1 as well as the new information in this chapter to define three customer types (those who shop at A, B, and C stores). (Use the form shown in Figure 2.5 on page 30 to record your research.)

In addition to the demographic and statistical information supplied in Chapter 1, you should conduct additional research in the area of psychographics. Psychographics explores the primary motivation for an individual's purchasing behaviors or the psychology behind their buying.

There are many marketing research organizations that provide this type of information; one of the most well-respected research companies is SRI Consulting and Business Intelligence. They have developed an eight-segment framework that profiles adult consumers into two dimensions: their primary motivation and their resources. An individual's primary motivation directs what he or she finds meaningful in the world or about him- or herself. Consumers are motivated or inspired by one of the three motivators: ideals, achievement, and self-expression. How an individual consumes resources is a by-product of his or her personality. SRI has developed a survey called VALS to measure the underlying psychological motivations of consumers, and to examine the resources that these consumers share in common. VALS is based on the belief that energy, intellectualism, self-confidence, innovativeness, impulsiveness, leadership, and vanity play a significant role in the consumption of merchandise (see Figures 2.1, 2.2, and 2.3).

The VALS survey predicts each group's typical consumption behaviors on the basis of those personality traits that affect behavior in the marketplace. VALS uses psychology to segment people according to their distinct personality traits rather than how much money they make or what they do for a living.

The eight VALS segments are *Innovators, Thinkers, Achievers, Experiencers, Believers, Strivers, Makers,* and *Survivors. Innovators* are sophisticated customers with a take-charge attitude. They are open to new products and ideas, and have significant resources at their disposal. *Thinkers* are idealistic, practical consumers who value functionality and durability, and VALS considers them to be "satisfied, mature, comfortable, and reflective people who value order, knowledge, and responsibility." *Achievers* lead relatively conventional lives and are goal oriented with a strong commitment to family and career. VALS also describes *Achievers* as politically conservative, value conscious, and respectful of authority. Their purchases are motivated by symbols of success, and they are highly imitative of those they respect and whose opinions they value. *Experiencers* are avid consumers of fashion who focus on "looking good" and are motivated by self-expression as well as new and different items and services. *Believers* are conservative with traditional values who tend to "buy American." VALS characterizes *Believers* as loyal but price-sensitive consumers, while *Strivers* are trendy, fun-loving individuals seeking the approval of others. *Strivers* also prefer stylish items, and imitate individuals who have more resources or are better off financially. *Makers* are practical and value self-sufficiency while expressing their individuality. They are generally not impressed with material possessions and prefer value to luxury. According to VALS, the final group, *Survivors,* are cautious consumers because of their limited resources, and prefer the familiar as they attempt to meet just the most basic needs.

SIMULATION:

Go to www.sric–bi.com/VALS/types.shtml.

Take the VALS survey and report your personal profile to your division merchandising manager (DMM). Buyers must be careful not to purchase merchandise based on their own taste and buying preference rather than that of their departmental customer. If you understand your own buying motivations, you are less likely to confuse them with those of the Perry's customer.

VALS also employs an additional research method to determine where these consumer segments live as identified by their ZIP codes. This method is called GeoVALS. This provides a retail buyer with key target consumer information for his or her trading area by linking consumer profiles to specific ZIP codes. GeoVALS can estimate potential sales performance by location, and define the merchandise mix based on the concentration of the consumer segment. SRI has provided GeoVALS lifestyle information on the on the CD-ROM for your use in developing your consumer profile.

History and Methodology

VALS™ pioneered the quest for greater consumer understanding.

Arnold Mitchell was a consumer futurist who wanted to explain the fragmentation of U.S. society in the 1960s and the implications for the economy and society. His work led to the development of the original VALS™ system as a model to explain various attitudes toward society and institutions. This work drew the attention of visionary marketers who encouraged Mitchell to enhance and extend his work as a marketing tool. SRI International formally inaugurated the VALS program in 1978, which led to a 1983 best-selling book, *Nine American Lifestyles*. *Advertising Age* cited VALS as "one of the ten top market research breakthroughs of the 1980s." Mitchell's pioneering method of applying psychographics to business management and marketing research led marketers to become interested in VALS as a way of thinking of consumers beyond demographics.

VALS™ evolved to explain the relationship between psychology and consumer behavior.

In the late 1980s the original VALS system's ability to predict consumer behavior was weakening as attitudes evolved. The VALS team realized that it should make improvements. From 1986 to 1989, the team built a new system to maximize the ability to predict consumer behavior using psychology as a more stable platform. A team from SRI International, Stanford University, and the University of California, Berkeley, determined that individual differences affect purchase behavior more directly than do societal trends and that consumer personality dimensions are more stable over time than shared values and beliefs.

A new VALS system emerged. Still grounded in the philosophy that mind-set and demographics are more powerful than demographics alone, VALS now uses psychology to describe the dynamics underlying consumer preferences and choices.

The current VALS system also incorporates a resource dimension and focuses less on social maturation than did the original system. Consumers are constrained in their full expression of self through behavior and purchase. So VALS also measures a person's ability to express himself or herself in the marketplace.

VALS™ identifies the psychological motivations that predict consumer differences.

The foundation of the VALS approach is that behavior is controlled by relatively independent psychological traits. VALS uses proprietary psychometric techniques to measure concepts that researchers have proved empirically to correlate with consumer behavior. The inherent stability of the system 15 years after its development is testimony to the theories of the development team.

FIGURE 2.1   VALS system

The Framework

Motivations and resources determine how a person will express himself or herself in the marketplace.

People buy products and services and seek experiences that fulfill their characteristic preferences and give shape, substance, and satisfaction to their lives. An individual's primary motivation determines what in particular about the self or the world is the meaningful core that governs his or her activities. VALS™ isolates the patterns that reinforce and sustain a person's identity as the person expresses it in the marketplace.

Some consumers choose what is "best."

Individuals motivated by *ideals* are grounded in knowledge and principles. For some people, this motivation is manifest in intellectual curiosity and quiet philosophical searching. For others, it expresses in an adherence to a personal or social code of conduct, such as religious, moral, or ethical convictions. In either case, the tendency is to base decisions on abstract, idealized criteria such as quality, integrity, and tradition.

Others are motivated by symbols of success.

People who are motivated by *achievement* strive for a clear social position. They seek explicit responsibilities and approval from a valued social group. Their focus is often on collective activities, such as those at work and with family, and on positive evaluation and reward. They base their choices on the expected reactions, concerns, and desires of people in the groups to which they belong or aspire to belong.

And some are driven by experience.

Individuals motivated by *self-expression* value actions for their impact on the physical world or the pleasure and excitement associated with them. A vital, emotional attachment to experiences is typical of this primary motivation, as is resistance to social controls that threaten experimentation and self-reliance. These action-oriented consumers make choices that emphasize individuality and personal challenge.

Psychological attributes strongly influence a person's ability and desire to buy.

A person's tendency to consume goods and services extends beyond age, income, and education. Energy, self-confidence, intellectualism, novelty seeking, innovativeness, impulsiveness, leadership, and vanity play a critical role. These personality traits in conjunction with key demographics determine an individual's resources. Different levels of resources enhance or constrain a person's expression of his or her primary motivation. The resource dimension gives VALS a hierarchical design, with the segments at the top of the map having a greater impact in the marketplace.

FIGURE 2.2   VALS framework

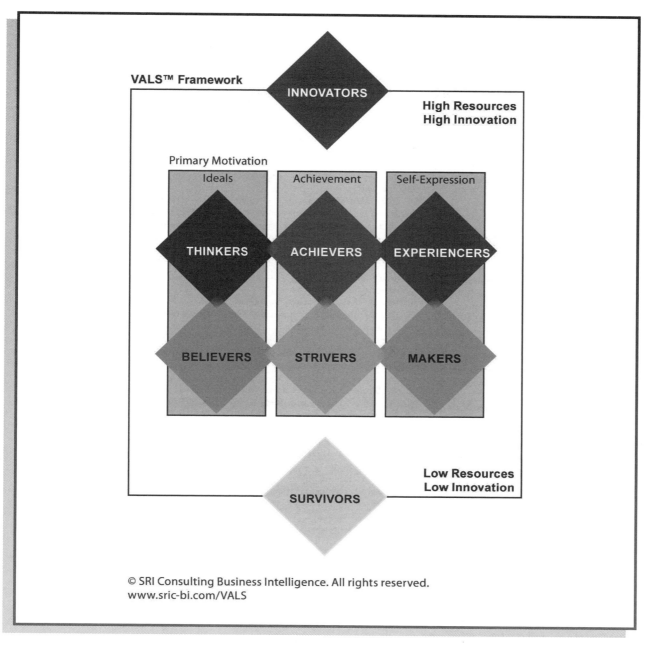

FIGURE 2.3   VALS types

CULTURAL DIFFERENCES

With the constant shifting of demographics in metropolitan and suburban areas of the United States, retail buyers must be in tune with the cultural changes in their marketplace. For example, if a shift in population indicates a significant increase in the number of Hispanic consumers, a buyer must understand the implications of a multicultural marketplace. According to the quarterly publication *Lifestyle Monitor*, Hispanic women between the ages of 25–34 spend more money on apparel than

La Vida Latina

Experts agree that Latinas look for styles in fashion that reflect their culture, and who better to look to than a Latina celebrity's own fashion line?

The Latina consumer is a hot commodity for apparel retailers in the U.S., and more and more major retailers are making moves to appeal to this audience.

Over the past 12 months, some of the biggest names in the mid-line department store channel have signed exclusive deals with well-known Latinas and given them a namesake fashion brand. Among those retail powerhouses are Sears, Kohl's and Kmart, which all inked deals with Latina personalities—Lucy Pereda, Daisy Fuentes and Thalia Sodí respectively. A smart move? Absolutely, for several compelling reasons: According to the most recent figures from Cotton Incorporated's Lifestyle Monitor, Hispanic women shop for apparel longer than any other ethnic group surveyed, spending an average of 127.65 minutes in the store. However, they shop less frequently, averaging only 2.11 times per month in 2003.

"Shopping represents entertainment for many Hispanic women," says Dr. Felipe Korzenny, professor of Hispanic Marketing Communication, Florida State University, and co-founder of Cheskin, a consulting and research firm specializing in cultural marketing. "They enjoy the experience when they engage in it, thus the longer episodes."

Victoria Sanchez-Lincoln, fashion director of *Latina* magazine, agrees with Dr. Korzenny's assessment, but also thinks there's a social element involved. "Latinas love to go shopping with friends and family and make a whole day of it," she says.

Hispanic female respondents to the Monitor research also cite that department stores are their preferred shopping destinations, followed by mass merchants and chain stores.

"At a department store, they can find all they need to outfit their entire family, kids, husbands and themselves," says Sanchez-Lincoln. "And they'll be drawn to stores that are offering merchandise and styles that are most appealing to them—Kohl's has Daisy Fuentes now and Kmart has Thalia Sodí's line," she adds.

When asked what makes these signature lines more appealing than other proprietary brands, Latina's Sanchez-Lincoln says it's all about the details.

"When Hispanic women go shopping for apparel, they're looking for styles with special details like embroidery, unique stitching and glitter—anything that makes a piece more special and will spice up their wardrobe," says Sanchez-Lincoln. "And color, bright bold colors and prints are very important."

Monitor data also shows that 40% of Latinas buy the latest fashions at the beginning of the season, making them the most likely group to do so. Notes Melissa Bastos, Cotton Incorporated manager, market analysis, "In an era of apparel price deflation, retailers are looking for niche markets that will assist in maximizing the bottom line. The success of private labels in niche markets, such as plus sizes and different ethnic groups, offers greater margins for stores. When given the choice, Latinas are willing to spend 15% more (than other consumers) of an extra $500 on apparel—which makes them an attractive shopper in the industry."

"Hispanics are very concerned with fashion and the latest trends. Our research shows this is true for Hispanics more than any other group," says Korzenny.

"Hispanic women like to mix up their fashion," affirms Sanchez-Lincoln. "They go from evening wear to very casual in their wardrobes, maybe pairing a unique, dressy top with jeans or other basics. The Latina woman likes to stand out, but she wants to be very feminine, too."

Experts agree that Latinas look for styles in fashion that reflect their culture, and who better to look to than a Latina celebrity's own fashion line?

Maria Seyrig, brand manager for Kmart Corporation, notes that the Thalia Sodí line, which rolled out in 335 of their 1,500 stores in August of last year, has been very well received and is exceeding expectations.

"Hispanic consumers make up more than 17 percent of Kmart's total sales, so the Thalia Sodí Collection was a natural fit with both our diverse customer base and our family of exclusive brands," says Seyrig. "The Thalia Sodí brand reflects a lifestyle that is active, passionate, bold, fashion conscious and original. It captures much of Thalia's personal style and has been inspired by her culture."

Says Tawn Earnest, spokesperson for Wisconsin-based Kohl's Department Stores, "Daisy Fuentes has developed modern options that make fashion simple and appeal to all women who like confident looks that reflect their personalities. Research shows that Daisy has a broad appeal to Kohl's customers, including Hispanics."

Although, according to the Monitor, Hispanic women are the least likely of all groups to browse for clothing online with only 27% saying they do so, retailers see it as a growing category and are putting considerable marketing effort into reaching this audience.

Sears has taken a likely next step in the courting of Latina consumers with the launch of their signature Lucy Pereda line.

The company has taken their Hispanic-focused marketing strategy into cyberspace on SearsenEspanol.com — where the Pereda line is a prominent feature on the all-Spanish language homepage. Kmart is also marketing the Thalia line on its Web site but they do so in English only.

"I think retailers want to catch women in their transition to the Internet. The more acculturated are already there, but others are slowly learning how to appreciate shopping online," says Dr. Korzenny.

The overall lesson for retailers is that merchandising and marketing with the Hispanic consumer in mind is key for attracting this burgeoning market segment.

Reproduced with permission of Cotton Incorporated

(http://www.cottoninc.com/LifeStyleMonitor/LSMSpring04/?Pg=9)

FIGURE 2.4   "La Vida Latina," *Lifestyle Monitor*, Cotton, Inc.

Caucasian women and shop more often (Solomon, 2004). Using this example, it would benefit a buyer (and his or her company) to find the styles and brands that young Hispanic women prefer. The buyer should also consider whether there are any differences in color or style preferences or size ranges based on culture and ethnicity.

SIMULATION:

GeoVALS Information

Refer to your CD-ROM for the GeoVALS information to secure demographic and statistical data and to obtain appropriate publications for your research. With this information and additional research, complete three worksheets in Figure 2.5, one each for an A, B, and C store. (See Worksheet 1 on the CD-ROM.)

Your consumer profiles should include the following information:

Average age of purchaser (not necessarily consumer)
Family income
Average purchase in dollars and units
GeoVALS Profile
Buying behaviors
Cultural implications

_____ Store

Average Age of Purchaser _____

Family Income _____

Average Purchase in Dollars and in Units _____

VALS Profile

Buying Behaviors

Cultural Implications

FIGURE 2.5   Perry's consumer profile worksheet

CHAPTER 3

STEP TWO

Research Current Trends

IN THIS CHAPTER, YOU WILL LEARN:

* The type of information buyers need to become experts in their industry
* The resources used to research various fashion and giftware industries

Your next step is to become an authority on your industry as quickly as possible. This involves researching current fashion trends, industry characteristics, and business news.

Two leading global resources that retailers, manufacturers, designers, marketing agencies, and public relation firms subscribe to are Worth Global Style Network (WGSN) and Marketing Directions, Inc. WGSN online offers an abundance of worldwide information on trend analysis, industry news, trade shows, etc. Markets covered include women's wear, men's wear, children's wear, fashion accessories, and home fashion. The service is based in London with international satellite offices around the world. Marketing Directions, Inc., based in the United States, is the international leader in home furnishings and is known for its trend- forecasting reports and consulting services. The service publishes the newsletter *The Trend Curve*™ six times a year to keep clients abreast of latest trends in the market. The *Connecting the Dots* blog includes the latest information as editor Michelle Lamb travels around the world.

There are many trade and business publications that offer information on fashion trends and retail statistics to provide guidance and direction to the retail buyer. A few sources[*] are:

TRADE PUBLICATIONS:
Women's Wear Daily (*WWD*)
Home Furnishings News (*HFN*)

*See Appendix A and the CD-ROM for a more extensive list of sources for industry information.

Chain Store Age
Inside Retailing
STORES

BUSINESS PUBLICATIONS:

American Demographics
Business Week
Forbes
Fortune
Wall Street Journal

Industry characteristics cover information particular to a market. A buyer must know what categories of merchandise and sizes are pertinent for the department. Apparel and accessories for one area are quite different from that of another area (e.g., Florida versus North Dakota). This is the same for market dates and trade show locations. It may be crucial for a young men's buyer to travel to the MAGIC show held in Las Vegas every February and August, but a home furnishings buyer may tell you that the Atlanta trade shows held in January and July are the most important. In the apparel industry, purchase terms of 8/10 EOM (end of the month) may be quoted, while terms of net 30 would be quoted in the tabletop market. Does the buyer of a particular area travel domestically only or internationally as well? What percentage of his or her department's merchandise is regular-priced and what percentage is promotional? What proportion of the merchandise selection should be fashion-forward or basic? Certain brands may be vital to set the status of the department.

Industry statistics are included on the CD-ROM. Other good sources for obtaining information include:

> Retail store buyers or assistant buyers
> Retail store department managers
> Manufacturer sales representatives

Using a minimum of five sources, write and submit a report on your specific industry. Your report should be in outline form, covering the following topics and format:

1. Market dates and delivery time line for the upcoming year

2. Market and trade show locations

3. Characteristics unique to the industry

4. Typical terms of purchase

5. Lead time on both domestic and foreign goods

6. Standard manufacturer *return-to-vendor (RTV)* policies and vendor merchandise exchange policies

7. Cooperative advertising agreements (bill enclosures, magazine, etc.)

8. Off-price and promotional merchandise

9. Fashion trends in:
   a. Classifications
   b. Subclassifications
   c. Colors
   d. Fabrications/material

10. Major vendors for each classification

11. Market trends (imports, licensed characters, etc.)

CHAPTER 4

STEP THREE

Develop Buying Plan

IN THIS CHAPTER, YOU WILL LEARN:

* To prepare a six-month dollar merchandise plan
* The concept behind the 4-5-4 calendar
* To become confident in estimating plan figures
* To analyze last year's figures and competitive operating results
* To calculate open-to-buy

The new buyer puts together a six-month dollar merchandise plan to spend available money correctly. The department's sales history is analyzed, along with current economic and fashion forecasts. Principles of planning sales and markdowns are introduced.

Now that you have obtained significant knowledge and background information about your industry, it is time to prepare your six-month dollar merchandise plan. The purpose of this plan is to budget your dollars that will be spent on merchandise in relation to your projected sales. The goal of every department is to plan the right merchandise in the right quantity at the right price in the right place at the right time.

The six-month dollar merchandise plan concentrates on the right quantity at the right price at the proper time. It plans merchandise in dollars, not by style or color.

Although the plan format may vary from one retail organization to another, the components remain the same. These components are:

1. Planned sales

2. Planned beginning-of-the-month (BOM) stock

DEPT. NAME _____   DEPT. # _____

BUYER _____

FALL		AUGUST	SEPTEMBER	OCTOBER	NOVEMBER	DECEMBER	JANUARY	FEBRUARY	SEASON TOTAL
SALES $	Last Year	$225.00	300.00	210.00	255.00	390.00	120.00		1,500.00
	Plan								
	% Inc/Dec	-100.0%	-100.0%	-100.0%	-100.0%	-100.0%	-100.0%		-100.0%
	Revised								
	Actual								
STOCK/SALES RATIO	Last Year	3.9	3.0	4.1	3.6	2.5	6.3	5.7	
	Plan								
BOM STOCK $ (Retail)	Last Year	$877.50	900.00	861.00	918.00	975.00	756.00	850.00	876.80 avg.
	Plan								
	Revised								
	Actual								
MARKDOWNS $	Last Year	$ 89.5	45.0	66.0	51.5	134.0	64.0		450.0
	Plan								
	% to Sales								
	% by Month								100.0%
	Revised								
	Actual								
PURCHASES $ (Retail)	Last Year	$337.00	306.00	333.00	363.50	305.00	278.00		1,922.50
	Plan								
	Revised								
	Actual								

SEASON TOTAL	LAST YEAR	PLAN	ACTUAL
Sales	$1,500.00	0.0	
Markup %	55%		
Markdown %	30%		
Gross Margin %	41.5%		
Average Stock	876.8	0.0	
Turnover	1.71		
NOTES:			

FIGURE 4.1   Perry's six-month dollar plan

3. Planned markdowns

4. Planned purchases

Note that there are many different formats for six-month plans, usually designed by the individual store. Figure 4.1 shows Perry's six-month dollar plan format. (See Worksheet 2 on the CD-ROM.)

SIMULATION:

Go to Figure 4.1 in the book or Worksheet 2 on the CD-ROM.

As is any budget, the six-month plan is a guideline to help the buyer spend dollars wisely. The objectives are to:

1. Decrease dollars invested in inventory

2. Increase turnover (number of times merchandise is restocked in a given period)

3. Control open-to-buy (money available to purchase additional merchandise)

4. Allow for improvement over last year's figures

5. Reduce loss of sales due to understocked merchandise

6. Improve gross margin

7. Provide a point of reference for comparing actual results to planned performance

The buyer begins with planning projected sales by month, usually for a six-month period, for either the spring/summer or fall/holiday season. These plans coincide with the retail-accounting calendar, or the 4-5-4 calendar, used by many department stores and depicted in Figure 4.2. This retail-accounting or fiscal calendar provides continuity by expressing seasons in "comparative selling" weeks and months.

The 4-5-4 calendar segments each quarter into three periods—four weeks in period I, five weeks in period II, and four weeks in period III—hence the name 4-5-4 calendar.

Six-month merchandise plans usually run February through July and August through January. Each season has 26 weeks, or two 13-week quarters.

Planned sales are the most significant element of the buyer's plan because they are the basis for all other elements of the entire budgeting process (BOM stock, markdowns, etc.).

The buyer uses his or her experience and market knowledge to make accurate sales forecasts. Research is a necessary component of forecasting and should include:

1. Local, regional, and national economic information

2. Sales trends

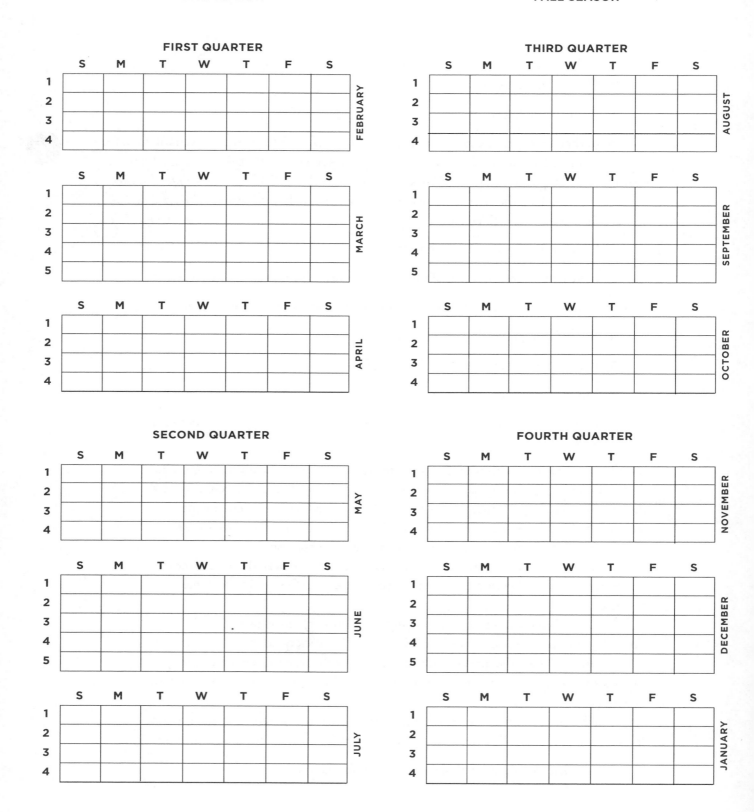

FIGURE 4.2   Fiscal year 4-5-4 accounting calendar

3. Fashion trends

4. Previous year's sales performance

Considering these factors, a buyer (with input from upper management) might forecast a sales increase or decrease, or for sales to remain "flat" (maintaining the same amount of sales as the previous year's season).

EXAMPLE:

After considering an inflation factor of 4% and local income growth of 5%, a buyer determines an 8% minimal increase in sales over last year's sales total of $1.5 million. What would the projected sales be for the next year?

$$
\begin{array}{rr}
\$1,500,000 & \$1,500,000 \\
\times \quad .08 & + \quad 120,000 \\
\hline
\$ \quad 120,000 & \$1,620,000 \\
\end{array}
$$

The buyer's next step is to break down this sales increase by month for the six-month period.

For example, if planning for August through January, the buyer would plan for sales to increase, decrease, or to remain flat for each month based on last year's sales figures and on current economic conditions.

Estimating is not an exact science. After a buyer considers all possible factors that could impact the business, he or she makes an educated guess. There is no one right answer. A group of buyers, given the same past history and current information, are likely to arrive at different forecasts based on individual perceptions and interpretations. But as long as the buyer can justify the forecast, management is likely to approve the figures.

PLANNING SALES

Your first step in planning the budget for your department is to determine your sales for the fall/holiday six-month period, August through January. Department stores belonging to a buying group or office are provided with the past year's statistics from member stores. Buyers can compare their department's performance related to stock turnover, stock-to-sales ratios, monthly sales distribution, markdowns, and so on, with both median and par performances of other comparable stores.

What's Ahead
for the Retail Industry

Susan Reda, Executive Editor

If only predicting the future were as simple as consulting a Magic 8 Ball.

Will mini-skirts make a comeback? *Outlook not so good.*

Should I open 25 new stores this year? It is decidedly so.

Will consumers buy beverages that promise to make them more beautiful? Don't count on it.

Fortunately, the editors of *STORES* don't quite trust the portable oracle the way they did when they were younger. And, we're betting that executives don't put much faith in the plastic fortune-telling orb, either.

Instead, in our annual effort to spot trends that will influence retailing in the coming year, we've listened intently, read ferociously and tried to think deep thoughts. Though we'll be the first to admit that we don't have all the answers, here are some predictions about issues and events we believe will shape the industry in 2008.

Bucking Recession

Are you afraid to say the "R" word? Plenty of economists are hesitating, too, and with good reason. While it's difficult to squelch the sentiment that the economy is on shaky ground, financial indicators are volatile—thus making predictions tricky business. Consumer spending has proven resilient enough to pull the nation through some rough patches in the past, and will sustain the economy in the coming year. A healthy dose of tentative optimism will be prudent for retailers during the first half of the year; as the nation gets closer to the 2008 election, a rebound may be in the offing.

Sanguine soothsayers claim that the Federal Reserve's interest-rate reductions over the past two months are enough to stave off recession and spark a return to a brisker business pace. They point out that the U.S. economy grew 3.9 percent in the third quarter and added 166,000 jobs in October, and reiterate Alan Greenspan's remarks that he sees "less than 50-50" odds of a U.S. recession.

Still, optimists don't make good press and bad news is having a bull run. Dispirited consumers, falling home values, and the sub-prime mortgage crisis are catalysts. And a slowdown in consumer spending, rising oil and gasoline prices and a slip in manufacturing activity are also shaking convictions.

For the retail industry, it all comes down to consumer confidence and how those feelings influence spending. Will shoppers continue to spend far more than they save? Will they shift their store preferences to align with a truncated budget?

The answer is probably "both." If anxious Americans decide to save or pay down debt rather than spend, retailers will take it on the chin. And, shoppers worried about the deepening housing downturn may feel that pulling equity out of their homes is no longer an option. Still, business at high-end and luxury retail stores has proven to be remarkably resilient. Indeed, shoppers behave differently today than they did in the past—making consumer behavior one of the most volatile factors in the economic equation.

There's truth to the argument that consumers keep on spending no matter what, and retailers can find solace there. The Neiman's shopper may trade down to a department store, and Kohl's shoppers may head for Target, but they'll keep spending. Quick-serve restaurants could be in for a lift; and fast feeders, like the comeback kid McDonald's, may see a revenue boost, too.

Green v. Green

Retail CEOs will find themselves faced with some hard questions about the green movement sweeping through corporate America. The biggest one: Can they be profit-driven and still be passionate about the planet?

Despite the best of intentions, most will find themselves in agreement with Kermit the Frog: It's not easy being green.

Converting lighting, providing reusable bags and establishing a recycling program are first steps on the road to becoming an eco-warrior. But building green stores, overhauling sourcing and manufacturing to be more in sync with green objectives and determining the right mix of green products on the shelf are a whole lot harder to do.

Wall Street says it stands ready to reward companies that back the environmental trend, but make no mistake—it's keeping a wary eye on the cost/benefit equation. And shoppers may say they're all for eco-friendly wares, but studies have shown that acceptance seems contingent on price. If 2008 brings about corporate and consumer belt-tightening, "green" could get squeezed.

That said, retailers have made impressive strides. Wal-Mart, JCPenney, Staples, Gap, Macy's, Office Depot, Whole Foods, Home Depot, REI: all have won kudos for their commitment to sustainability. Look for those

efforts to continue in '08—provided these companies continue to see ROI. The next big efforts will be a push to achieve greater social responsibility in sourcing and to install more environmentally friendly networking and storage equipment on the IT side.

Attention Small Mart Shoppers

For a long time it was all about "big"—big stores, deep product offerings, expansive thinking. Now the tide has turned: Retail executives are not only thinking small, they're building smaller stores, delivering edited product assortments and betting that this approach will deliver a big return on investment.

Nowhere is that more apparent than in the supermarket channel. Since Tesco announced its British invasion last year, the spotlight has been on stores of the 10,000-sq.-ft. variety. Safeway's chairman is prepared to open smaller stores if Tesco's Fresh & Easy Neighborhood Market clicks. Wal-Mart has registered two new trademarks and is expected to test a convenience store format in Southern California, where they've struggled to overcome big-box opposition. Whole Foods announced intentions to convert a former Wild Oats store in Colorado to a Whole Foods Market Express.

Food retailers are not the only ones hip to being small. Circuit City is adding smaller-scale The City stores to its mix, and Tiffany & Co. will open 2,000-sq.-ft. "Collections" shops. JCPenney is trying smaller, off-mall shops, and Best Buy is opening units that are up to 40 percent smaller than its current stores.

Rewriting the Rules of Engagement

These days shoppers can connect to just about anyone, anywhere at anytime. Expect that increased visibility to rewrite the rules of engagement for retailers and marketers.

We're fast approaching a time when entire cities will be wireless. Hot spots are already commonplace, and the next generation of wireless (802.11n) promises to re-engineer access in environments such as retail stores, where the use of multiple devices creates multiple hurdles. What all that means is that more shoppers will be splitting their time between looking at the device in their hands and looking at the shelves.

And that assumes they're visiting your store. The always-on generation, which is moving into its prime spending years, doesn't always see the need to visit a store. Its members use their social networking skills to determine whether an item is worth buying, then complete that purchase using their cell phone or other electronic device. In 2008, retailers will need to ask

FIGURE 4.3   "What's Ahead for the Retail Industry," Susan Reda, *STORES* themselves: Am I really a multi-channel retailer if I'm not making product available via the mobile web?

Look for one of the "it" applications for '08 to be Mobile Social Software (MoSoSo) tools that connect people through wireless phones using location-based services. They've been around for a while (with mixed results), but as Facebook and MySpace become omnipresent and Google's plans for OpenSocial take root, MoSoSo apps will quickly become the de facto standard.

These data-rich experiences cast a blinding spotlight on the need for greater business intelligence; managing data more effectively and making it actionable will be synonymous with success.

Steady Doses of Inconsistency

You know this guy, right? Installed solar panels on the roof of his home; insists on cutting his grass with a push mower; recycles with vengeance. Yet, parked in his driveway is a Hummer. Having trouble putting the pieces together? That's the challenge retailers and marketers face.

Companies that can figure out how to cater to consumers' paradoxical desires have the best chance to succeed.

The purchasing paradox weaves together trends and counter trends; customers want to fit in with the crowd, own the latest must-have gadget, but at the same time they want to customize their purchases. Inconsistency reigns supreme: the woman who carries a Coach handbag and buys only organic meat and produce insists she never pays full-price for apparel.

The consumer economy remains split by the haves and have nots, and this dichotomy will grow more pronounced in 2008. High-end luxury and couture fashion may weather economic hits, but just about everyone else is in for a very bumpy ride.

Today's consumer is best defined as the choice generation. They hold the power to TiVo past your ads, batch delete your e-mails and opt out of everything from telemarketing calls to newsletters. Finding ways to connect with them will be one of the greatest challenges of the coming year.

Exclusivity Meets Authenticity

Consumers are tired of seeing the same thing from one store to the next. Look for exclusive brands, partnerships and the like to reach critical mass in 2008 as retailers look to break free from the boredom of sameness, delivering exclusive products and fostering partnerships that set their brand apart.

Target started the trend with precisely timed offerings presented from up-and-coming designers. Macy's has been carving its niche with a commitment to celebrity brands and recently announced an exclusive partnership with Tommy Hilfiger. And Wal-Mart is the exclusive retail distributor of The Eagles' first CD of new music in 28 years.

Private brands returned in a big way in 2007; now the challenge is for retailers to make sure shoppers know how special these collections are.

Exclusivity doesn't have to occur solely within the four walls of the main store: Safeway quietly opened a restaurant called Citrine earlier this year, and American Eagle is dabbling in the lingerie specialty arena with aerie, a spin-off of one of its private brands. Shoppers are always looking for something new, opportunities abound for businesses willing to step outside their comfort zones.

Whatever retailers and marketers do, they need to keep it real—or, to borrow the buzzword of the day, "authentic." Shoppers are way too savvy to lap up a phony marketing facade, and they're already becoming skeptical of online reviews and blogs.

Strip away the noise, provide expert information structured in a usable way—and be brave enough to add other authentic voices to the mix. Today's consumer looks for brands that share her passion—whether it is for a charity, a lifestyle or some other cause. That's why the Dove marketing campaign resonated so strongly with women; it's also why a chain like Trader Joe's has managed to cultivate such unshakeable customer loyalty. Its employees live and breathe the brand's equity, and shoppers get that.

Born in the USA Redux

Springsteen's familiar anthem had nothing to do with products manufactured in the good 'ol USA, but expect Americans—wary of tainted toothpaste, lead-laden toys and contaminated foods—to make it a rallying cry in 2008.

While there's little evidence that "Made in the USA" will make a stunning comeback anytime soon, there are clear signs that Americans are paying more attention to where goods are sourced, where ingredients come from and how products move through the supply chain.

As shoppers become more discerning, opportunities intensify for retailers to deliver the information shoppers want. Make it easy for pet owners to identify where the food they're about to buy was manufactured. Tell them where the seafood you're selling comes from, and assure parents that the toys they're buying aren't colored with high-lead-content paints.

Retailers and manufacturers that source products locally—such as Whole Foods' commitment to local farmers, and a handful of apparel manufacturers that continue to make goods stateside—are likely to see a surge in business as shoppers become more aware of these associations and respond favorably.

Waiting to Exhale

Know anyone who strolls the mall these days? Probably not. Shoppers' opportunities to buy a new shade of lipstick or a fetching pair of pumps are likely to be sandwiched between a doctor's appointment and their kid's soccer game. Since Americans young, old and in between are busier and more stressed out than ever before, it's up to retailers to ease tensions associated with shopping.

How can retailers cater to consumers who don't linger long enough to look over all they have to offer? The answers vary depending on the store, but how about:

* Offering shoppers a small bottle of water

* Making sure signs are clear and your stores are easy to navigate

* Never allowing a checkout line to get more than two deep before opening another register

* Offering shoppers standing in line a sample of a new food item, or a coupon for 10 percent off one item.

* Do something that tells the shopper "your time matters to me"—or risk having them drop their purchases in a heap and head for the door.

Look for curbside delivery by quick-service restaurants to snowball to other food retailers. Expect a proliferation of retail spa services to spring up at the mall. Watch for an explosion of health clinics in drug store settings as Walgreens, CVS and the rest use their keen location strategy to simplify treatment of minor ailments and deliver a healthy dose of goodwill.

Finally, efforts to simplify and multi-task at the same time (there's that paradox again) will be rewarded. Think of the success of lifestyle malls. They provide shoppers a chance to pick up jeans at the Gap and buy a gift from Pottery Barn before relaxing for an hour at Cheesecake Factory.

Used with permission of *STORES Magazine*, published by the National Retail Federation. December 2007

FIGURE 4.3 (CONTINUED)

The factors you should consider in planning your six-month budget are:

1. Sales history of the department for the last year (see Figure 4.1)

2. Industry statistics

3. Fashion trends

4. Local Fredericksburg economy

5. National economics

6. Buying office's market report

You will need to research current economic indicators on retail growth to obtain information to estimate your department's sales growth (see Appendix A and the CD-ROM). An example of an appropriate source would be an article such as "What's Ahead for Retail Industry" (see Figure 4.3). This type of article will assist you in making an educated estimate regarding how much you might expect your departmental sales to increase or decrease.

Use Figure 4.4 to complete the sales plan, justifying your sales increase or decrease for your department. Remember that the fall/holiday season does a greater percentage of business than the spring/summer period. This is due to several factors, including shopping-intensive periods such as back-to-school, Christmas, and other holidays.

Once you have justified your sales increase or decrease, your next step is to break down your sales by month. Your considerations will be:

1. Last year's actual sales distribution (percentage of sales obtained each month in relation to season total)

2. Retail-accounting calendar, with adjustments for holidays and special promotions

3. Recommendations from Perry's buying office in monthly sales distribution (in percentages) for the upcoming fall/holiday season, as follows:

August	15%
September	18%
October	14%
November	17%
December	26%
January	10%
TOTAL	100%

Using Figures 4.4 and 4.5, plan your monthly sales for August through January. Calculate the increase or decrease of planned sales in relation to last year's actual figures, using the chart in Figure 4.6.

SIMULATION: *Go to Figures 4.4, 4.5, and 4.6 in the book or Worksheets 3, 4, and 5 on the CD-ROM.*

EXAMPLE:

August Last Year's Sales	$225,000
August Planned Sales	$235,000
Dollar Increase	$ 10,000

$$\text{Percent Increase} = \frac{\text{Dollar increase}}{\text{Last Year's sales}}$$

$$\text{Percent Increase} = \frac{\$10,000}{\$225,000} = 4.4\%$$

Remember to justify your analysis of your sales forecast by month.

PERRY'S

SALES INCREASE/DECREASE

Your Plan:

Percentage increase or decrease _____ %

Dollar increase or decrease $ _____

Justification

(Use as many pages as necessary to support your decision.)

FIGURE 4.4   Perry's sales plan worksheet

Planned monthly sales by percentage of season sales volume

MONTH	PERCENT	$\times$ SEASON SALES $	= MONTHLY SALES $
August	_____	_____	_____
September	_____	_____	_____
October	_____	_____	_____
November	_____	_____	_____
December	_____	_____	_____
January	_____	_____	_____

FIGURE 4.5   Perry's monthly sales plan

	AUGUST	SEPTEMBER	OCTOBER	NOVEMBER	DECEMBER	JANUARY
PL Sales						
LY Sales	225.0	300.0	210.0	255.0	390.0	120.0
$ Inc/Dec						
% Inc/Dec						

Justification by Month:

August

September

October

November

December

January

FIGURE 4.6 Perry's monthly sales increase/decrease

PLANNING BEGINNING-OF-THE-MONTH STOCK (BOM STOCK)

A buyer plans a beginning-of-the-month (BOM) stock sufficient to meet planned sales without overstocking the department. This is called a *balanced stock*. BOM inventory is used instead of end-of-the-month (EOM) stock because the BOM stock produces that month's sales. For example, January BOM stock is December's EOM stock. In other words, at 11:59 PM on December 31, the stock on the sales floor (December EOM) has the same value in dollars as on January 1 at 12:01 AM (January BOM).

There are several methods of planning inventories, but the one most widely seen in the industry and taught in classrooms is the stock-to-sales ratio method. This method requires the buyer to establish a relationship or ratio of stock (BOM) to sales on a monthly basis. For example, a buyer might determine from past records that in November there is a 4 to 1 ratio (expressed 4.0). That is, for every $1.00 of planned sales, $4.00 is invested in merchandise. The ratios will vary from month to month according to selling seasons, holidays, etc. Buyers consider these factors in establishing monthly stock-to-sales ratios:

* Department's previous performance

* Industry stock/sales ratios

After the stock/sales ratio or relationship is established, the buyer multiplies this ratio times the planned sales to find the BOM inventory needs in dollars.

EXAMPLE:

January planned sales = $10,000

$$\frac{\text{January stock}}{\text{sales ratio}} = 3.7$$

Planned sales × stock/sales ratio = BOM stock
$10,000 × 3.7 = $37,000 January BOM stock

TURNOVER

Turnover is the rate or velocity at which the average stock has been sold and the money earned reinvested into merchandise within a given period. Graphically expressed it looks like this:

Merchandise → $$ → Merchandise → 1 Turnover (1.0)

Turnover is significant to the buyer because it is a gauge of a department's efficiency and productivity. The buyer seeks a healthy turnover because it:

1. Ensures the influx of new, fresh merchandise

2. Lowers markdowns

3. Increases available dollars to purchase new merchandise (open-to-buy)

As a buyer, you can improve Perry's turnover rate by two direct methods: (1) increase sales, or (2) decrease dollars invested in merchandise. This relationship is expressed as indicated in the formula for turnover:

$$\text{Stock turnover} = \frac{\text{Net sales for a period}}{\text{Average inventory or stock for the same period}}$$

Average stock is merely the sum of the retail inventories divided by the number of inventories in the period examined (month, season, or year). The formula is:

$$\text{Average Stock} = \frac{\text{BOM stock for the given period}}{\text{\# of inventories (BOM stock)}}$$

EXAMPLE:

The average inventory for a year would be calculated by adding the 12 BOM inventories (January to December) plus the December EOM inventory, and then dividing this by 13 (the number of inventories examined).

January BOM	$	96,000
February BOM	$	93,500
March BOM	$	115,500
April BOM	$	126,000
May BOM	$	114,000
June BOM	$	114,000
July BOM	$	115,500
August BOM	$	127,500
September BOM	$	123,000
October BOM	$	130,500
November BOM	$	133,500

December BOM	$ 201,000
December EOM (January BOM)	$ 96,500
TOTAL	$ 1,586,500

$$\frac{\$1,586,500}{13} = \$122,038.46 \text{ average stock}$$

$$= \$122,038.00 \text{ (rounded off)}$$

To calculate average stock for the fall/holiday six-month period using the same example, add August BOM through January BOM stocks plus January EOM (February BOM), given as follows, and divide by 7 (the number of inventories).

EXAMPLE:

Sum of August BOM through January EOM	=	$ 812,000
January EOM (February BOM)	+	$ 94,000
Total of Inventories	=	$906,000

$$\frac{\$906,000}{7} = \$129,428.57 \text{ average stock}$$

$$= \$129,429 \text{ (rounded off)}$$

SIMULATION:

Go to Figure 4.7 in the book or Worksheet 6 on the CD-ROM.

The next step in completing your six-month plan is to establish your stock-to-sales ratios for your department and to multiply them by your planned sales for each corresponding month. Remember, your possible sources of information are previous departmental performance and industry stock-to-sales ratios.

Refer to Figure 4.1 for last year's figures. Use Figure 4.7 to record your stock-to-sales ratios and BOM stock. Justify the plans stock-to-sales ratios by month.

When using the stock-to-sales ratio method of planning stock, buyers often experience difficulty in arriving at the exact planned average stock. For this reason, some buyers prefer to distribute stock by month on a percentage-to-month basis. The season's average stock figure times 7 (number of inventories) equals 100. Each month is assigned a percentage of the total based on previous years' figures. For the purpose of this simulation, you have been provided only last year's figures.

EXAMPLE:

Sum of 7 months of stock = $1,500,000

August stock = $180,000

$$\frac{\text{Month stock}}{\text{Sum of 7 months of stock}} = \text{Month \% to total stock}$$

$$\frac{\$180,000}{\$1,500,000} = .12 \text{ or } 12\% \text{ of the total stock}$$

PLANNING MARKDOWNS

Markdowns are reductions in the retail price—a very necessary and inevitable element in fashion merchandising. They are multifunctional and a component of the six-month plan that a buyer must anticipate. The functions of markdowns are to:

1. Adjust pricing errors

2. Increase stock turnover

3. Correct buying errors

4. Remove out-of-season and/or broken assortment merchandise

5. Increase open-to-buy dollars (to allow the purchase of new merchandise)

6. Improve cash flow

7. Increase traffic within a store or department

These are the positive effects of markdowns, but the negative effects cannot be overlooked. These negative aspects include:

1. Reduction in net sales and, in turn, reduction in gross margin and profit

2. Creation of "promotional" image, based on consumer's expectations

In planning markdowns for the six-month plan, the buyer reviews last year's markdowns in dollars and as a percentage of actual sales.

The first step in planning markdowns is to establish an overall markdown percentage. This percentage is then multiplied by the total sales for the six-month period.

The next step is to distribute markdowns by month. To establish a percentage for each month of your six-month plan, use last year's markdown percent to sales figures

	AUGUST	SEPTEMBER	OCTOBER	NOVEMBER	DECEMBER	JANUARY	FEBRUARY
PL Sales	39.8	15.0	31.4	20.2	34.4	53.3	
S/S Ratio							
BOM Stock							

Plan Sales × Stock/Sales Ratio = BOM Stock

Justification by Month:

August

September

October

November

December

January

February (January EOM)

FIGURE 4.7   Perry's worksheet for stock/sales ratio and BOM stock

(Figure 4.1) as a guide. The monthly percentage multiplied by the monthly planned sales establishes the monthly planned markdowns.

Because monthly percentages to sales figures do not total 100 percent, buyers often distribute markdowns using the percentage-by-month formula. This formula establishes season total markdowns as 100 percent, and each month is a percentage of that total. Refer to last year's markdown figures by month in Figure 4.1.

The nature of the merchandise dictates the percentage of markdown, as does the time of the year. For example, the Christmas season is a strong regular-price selling season for lingerie and would dictate a later and less significant markdown than Christmas apparel and other seasonal goods. Most buyers would like to move their stock out of the store at the height of the season while customer traffic is heaviest. This can be accomplished with earlier and deeper markdowns.

Your next step is to review last year's markdowns, in both dollars and percentages, and industry averages. Last year's markdown figures by month can be found in Figure 4.1. Industry figures can be researched in trade publications or by calling industry buyers. These will be your basis for establishing your departmental markdowns in both dollars and percentages.

> **SIMULATION:**
> *Go to Figure 4.8 in the book or Worksheet 7 on the CD-ROM.*

The worksheet—Figure 4.8—will help you complete the next step of your six-month plan. Remember, first establish your percentage of markdown for each month of your plan.

Follow these steps:

1. Fill in plan sales by month and total.

2. Fill in total markdown dollars in the total markdown dollar column based on your established markdown percentage plan.

3. Distribute markdown percentage by month using last year's figures, listed below as a guideline.

4. Your markdown dollars will automatically calculate on the electronic spreadsheet after you add the percentage by month.

5. Your markdown sales percentage by month to sales will also be automatically calculated.

	AUGUST	SEPTEMBER	OCTOBER	NOVEMBER	DECEMBER	JANUARY	TOTAL
MD% to Sales	39.8	15.0	31.4	20.2	34.4	53.3	
MD% by Month	19.9	10.0	14.7	11.4	29.8	14.2	100.0

PLANNING PURCHASES

The basic elements of your plan have been established in your worksheets. You have planned your sales, stock, and markdowns. When entered into the following formula, they establish the dollars (at retail) available to purchase merchandise.

    Planned sales
+ Planned EOM stock (the next month's BOM stock)
+ Planned markdowns
– Planned BOM stock
_____
= Planned purchases at retail

Planned purchases can be converted into a cost figure by multiplying the planned purchases times the markup complement (100 percent minus the markup percent).

EXAMPLE:
Planned purchases = $100,000 (at retail)
MU% = 47%
$100,000 × (100% – 47%) =
$100,000 × .53 = $53,000 planned purchases at cost

SIMULATION: *Go to Figures 4.1 and 4.9 in the book or Worksheets 2 and 8 on the CD-ROM.*

You are now ready to calculate your planned purchases. Use the worksheet in Figure 4.9 to complete your six-month plan. You will need February's BOM to calculate January's planned purchases (February BOM = January EOM).

Calculate all your figures at retail and at cost.

After you have completed your six-month plan, you can calculate your average stock and your stock turnover for this six-month period.

All this information should be transferred to your formal plan in Figure 4.1.

OPEN-TO-BUY

Although it will not be necessary to calculate open-to-buy in this simulation, it is probably the most important concept in retail buying. Open-to-buy (OTB) is the check-and-balance system built into the six-month plan. It allows the buyer to regulate or adjust inventory levels according to actual sales. It acts as an escape valve. If sales are down in relation to the plan, adjustments can be made to the purchases to prevent overstocking. Of course, if sales exceed the plan, additional merchandise can be purchased to prevent an understocked selling floor.

	AUGUST	SEPTEMBER	OCTOBER	NOVEMBER	DECEMBER	JANUARY	TOTAL
PL Sales							
MD % to Sales							
MD $							
MD % by Month							0%

Plan Sales × MD % to Sales = MD $

Justification of Plan Markdowns by Month:

August

September

October

November

December

January

FIGURE 4.8   Perry's worksheet for plan markdowns

Open-to-buy is the number of dollars available to purchase merchandise that is not accounted for by previous purchase orders.

	Planned purchases	
–	Outstanding purchase orders not yet delivered	
=	Open-to-buy	

To understand this concept, we must look at the entire formula:

	Planned sales for August	$20,000
+	Planned EOM stock for August	$25,000
+	Planned markdowns for August	$ 500
=	Merchandise required	$45,500
	Merchandise required	$45,500
–	Planned BOM stock for August	$25,000
=	Planned purchases for August	$20,500
–	On order for August	$15,500
=	Open-to-buy for August	$ 5,000

As we already know, our six-month plan is completed well in advance of (four to six months) the season. The buyer in our example spent or placed orders for all but $5,000 of available money. If in July there is a downward trend in sales, with actual sales below plan by $3,000, the open-to-buy would decrease by the same amount.

	Actual sales	$ 17,000
+	EOM stock	$25,000
+	Markdowns	$ 500
=	Merchandise required	$42,500
–	BOM stock	$25,000
=	Purchases	$ 17,500
–	On order	$ 15,500
=	Open-to-buy	$ 2,000

This is the essence of inventory control. Available money is decreased to prevent overstocking. Remember, merchandise requirements are based on the relationship of stock to sales. Of course, this same system also works in a positive direction. If sales are beyond the buyer's projections, open-to-buy will increase proportionately.

	AUGUST	SEPTEMBER	OCTOBER	NOVEMBER	DECEMBER	JANUARY
Plan Sales						
(plus)						
Plan EOM Stock						
(plus)						
Plan MD						
(minus)						
Plan BOM						
(equals)						
Plan Purchases at Retail						
(times)						
100% – MU%						
(equals)						
Plan Purchases at Cost						

FIGURE 4.9   Perry's worksheet for plan purchases

CHAPTER 5

STEP FOUR

Develop Assortment Plan

IN THIS CHAPTER, YOU WILL LEARN:

* To analyze merchandise needs by classification, subclassification, fabrication, color, size, price points, and units
* To rank merchandise needs by percentage and dollars

In this chapter, the new buyer develops an assortment plan, which involves several tasks. They include reviewing the department's classifications, considering subclassifications, considering at aspects such as fabrication and color, determining sales by month, and calculating price points and price lines.

CLASSIFICATIONS

Department store buyers have the monumental task of budgeting large sums of money and determining how that money is to be spent. As do most wise financiers, they begin with a plan. This plan converts large sums of money into *classifications* of merchandise to be carried in their departments. This breakdown of merchandise by classification (e.g., pants, shirts, sweaters, for apparel) is called an *assortment plan*.

An assortment plan ultimately allows the buyer to examine the department from the perspective of merchandise needs in relation to style, fabrication, color, size, and price lines.

Your first step in developing an assortment plan is to review the classifications that presently exist in your department. The CD-ROM includes the classifications and the percentages of sales produced for last year's fall/holiday season in all four departments.

Table 5.1 is an example for a Boys 4–7 department.

TABLE 5.1

BOYS 4-7—CLASSIFICATIONS		
CLASSIFICATION	PERCENT	SALES IN THOUSANDS
Sweaters	6.0	$ 90.0
Knit Tops	20.0	$ 300.0
Shirts	6.0	$ 90.0
Suits & Dress Coats	5.0	$ 75.0
Pants	15.0	$ 225.0
Shorts	3.0	$ 45.0
Activewear & Swimwear	22.0	$ 330.0
Underwear & Socks	8.5	$ 127.5
Sleepwear	2.5	$ 37.5
Outerwear	9.0	$ 135.0
Accessories	2.0	$ 30.0
Miscellaneous	1.0	$ 15.0
TOTAL	100.0	$1,500.0

SIMULATION:
Go to Figure 5.1 in the book or Worksheet 9 on the CD-ROM and to your department's Industry Statistics on the CD-ROM.

You must decide if any additional classifications for new merchandise should be added or if dated classifications should be deleted. It is the job of the buyer to continually update classifications to remain current with the marketplace. Sales by classification should be reviewed to see how the marketplace and the consumer might adjust the percentage that each classification produces. Review your research and look through trade magazines to refresh your memory.

List your department's classifications in Figure 5.1. Next, determine what percentage of sales each classification accounts for in the total fall/holiday plan. Your percentages should equal 100 percent. To complete Figure 5.1, these percentages can be multiplied by the total planned sales for the fall/holiday season.

MONTHLY SALES BY CLASSIFICATION

Now that you have determined your season sales by classification, you need to distribute them by month. At this point, you will combine the monthly sales information already entered in your six-month plan in Figure 4.1 with sales by classification.

SALES BY CLASSIFICATION, PERCENTAGE, AND DOLLARS

CLASSIFICATION	PERCENT	×	SEASON SALES	=	CLASS SALES
_____	_____		_____		_____
_____	_____		_____		_____
_____	_____		_____		_____
_____	_____		_____		_____
_____	_____		_____		_____
_____	_____		_____		_____
_____	_____		_____		_____
_____	_____		_____		_____
_____	_____		_____		_____
_____	_____		_____		_____
TOTAL	**100%**				_____

FIGURE 5.1   Perry's sales by classification, percentage, and dollars

SIMULATION:

Go to Figure 5.2 in the book or Worksheet 10 on the CD-ROM.

Complete Figure 5.2 by following the steps detailed below. On the CD-ROM, Worksheet 10 is color-coded to help you understand what information is needed and where to transfer the information.

STEP 1   Using Figure 4.5 from the previous chapter, transfer the monthly sales distribution percentages to the top line of Figure 5.2. The sum of these percentages must equal 100 percent.

STEP 2   Using Figure 5.1, transfer all of the fall/holiday sales classifications (pants, shirts, etc.) into the designated spaces.

STEP 3   Using Figure 5.1, transfer the fall/holiday class sales into the last column.

STEP 4   List total sales in dollars by month across the bottom of the page. This figure also can be taken from Figure 5.1. Total monthly sales should equal sales plan for the season.

STEP 5   Multiply the monthly sales percent by each classification sales figure to get the monthly sales by classification. (The electronic worksheet contains spreadsheet formulas, so these highlighted figures should be calculated automatically.)

EXAMPLE:

If the classification of knit tops will produce 22% of the yearly sales of $1.3 million, then this equates to $286,000 (.22 × $1,300,000).

If August sales are 10% of yearly sales, then knit tops for August would be calculated as 10% × $286,000 = $28,600.

SUBCLASSIFICATIONS

Although the merchandise focus has narrowed, the dollar amounts by classification are still too large to provide accurate buying information. Your next step is to

SIMULATION:

Go to Figure 5.3 in the book or Worksheet 11 on the CD-ROM.

develop *subclassifications*. These subclassifications allow a buyer to be more precise in analyzing and forecasting the merchandise assortment. For example, a sweater classification could be further subdivided into crew, V-neck, henley, and cardigan. In some departments, classifications are not further separated into subclassifications. This is not the situation for departments in which buying is more specialized.

Using the form in Figure 5.3, develop subclassifications for one classification in your department.

	AUGUST	SEPTEMBER	OCTOBER	NOVEMBER	DECEMBER	JANUARY	TOTAL
PERCENT	_____	_____	_____	_____	_____	_____	100%

CLASS

_____	_____	_____	_____	_____	_____	_____	_____
_____	_____	_____	_____	_____	_____	_____	_____
_____	_____	_____	_____	_____	_____	_____	_____
_____	_____	_____	_____	_____	_____	_____	_____
_____	_____	_____	_____	_____	_____	_____	_____
_____	_____	_____	_____	_____	_____	_____	_____
_____	_____	_____	_____	_____	_____	_____	_____
_____	_____	_____	_____	_____	_____	_____	_____
_____	_____	_____	_____	_____	_____	_____	_____
_____	_____	_____	_____	_____	_____	_____	_____
_____	_____	_____	_____	_____	_____	_____	_____
TOTAL SALES	_____	_____	_____	_____	_____	_____	_____

FIGURE 5.2   Perry's classification sales by month

SUBCLASSIFICATIONS FOR _____ **CLASSIFICATION**

1. _____

2. _____

3. _____

4. _____

5. _____

6. _____

7. _____

8. _____

FIGURE 5.3   Perry's subclassifications

(Percentages based on total department sales)

FABRICATION:

Cotton and blends	82%
Polyester	4%
Acrylic	6%
Wool and blends	2%
Nylon	5%
Other	1%
	100%

COLOR:

White	23%
Black	12%
Blue/Navy	11%
Red	5%
Khaki	7%
Gray	4%
Fashion brights	5%
(purple, turquoise, fuschia, etc.)	
Pastels	3%
Patterns (prints, plaids)	30%
	100%

SIZE: (Based on prepack of 12 units)

4	2	S	3
5	4	M	5
6	4	L	4
7	2		12
	12		

VENDOR FOR BOY'S DENIM JEANS:

Carter's	15%
Oshkosh	10%
Levi's	25%
Guess	10%
Flapdoodles	5%
Good Lad	5%
Other, including private label	30%
	100%

FIGURE 5.4   Perry's Boys 4–7 Department assortment planning factors for last year

ASSORTMENT PLAN BY FABRICATION

FOR _____CLASSIFICATION

FABRICATION DISTRIBUTION   PERCENT TO TOTAL

_____   _____

_____   _____

_____   _____

_____   _____

_____   _____

_____   _____

_____   _____

_____   _____

_____   _____

100%

JUSTIFICATION:

FIGURE 5.5   Perry's assortment plan by fabrication

ASSORTMENT PLAN BY COLOR

FOR ———————— CLASSIFICATION

COLOR DISTRIBUTION
PERCENT TO TOTAL

————————————   ————————————

————————————   ————————————

————————————   ————————————

————————————   ————————————

————————————   ————————————

————————————   ————————————

————————————   ————————————

————————————   ————————————

————————————   ————————————

100%

JUSTIFICATION:

FIGURE 5.6   Perry's assortment plan by color

SIZE DISTRIBUTION   PERCENT TO TOTAL

_____   _____

_____   _____

_____   _____

_____   _____

_____   _____

_____   _____

_____   _____

_____   _____

_____   _____

                                     100%

JUSTIFICATION:

FIGURE 5.7   Perry's assortment plan by size

OTHER FACTORS IN ASSORTMENT PLANNING

Buyers analyze their merchandise needs by factors other than classifications and subclassifications. You should also consider fabrication, color, size, vendor and price lines. Figure 5.4 shows an example of last year's fall/holiday plan for these other factors in a Boys 4–7 pant classification. Use this only as a guide; your research will help you make adjustments for your new assortment plan.

You are now ready to plan your classification by fabrication, color, size, and vendors. Fill in the information on Figures 5.5, 5.6, 5.7, and 5.8.

SIMULATION: Go to Figures 5.5, 5.6, 5.7, and 5.8 in the book or Worksheets 12, 13, 14, and 15 on the CD-ROM.

PRICE LINES

The last step of the assortment plan is to determine how the buyer spends the budgeted dollars, both in units and by *price line*. Prior to completing this exercise, purchases should be distributed by classification.

To find the total purchases, refer to your six-month dollar plan in Figure 4.1, which you completed previously. Total planned purchases equal the six-month sum of August through January planned purchases. Transfer your total dollar purchases to the bottom line of Figure 5.9. Transfer the classification percentages from Figure 5.1 to Figure 5.9. Now multiply the classification percentage by the total dollar purchases to arrive at the total purchases by classification. When you have completed Figure 5.9, you will have a more accurate picture of the dollars available to spend by each classification.

SIMULATION: Go to Figures 4.1, 5.1, and 5.9 in the book or Worksheets 2, 9, and 16 on the CD-ROM.

The final use of the assortment plan is to determine how the buyer spends the budgeted dollars both in units and by price line. This procedure is illustrated in the following example:

EXAMPLE:

Class A	Price Line		# of Units	$ by Price Line
	$20	30%	_____	$ 85,800
	$25	50%	_____	$ 143,000
	$30	20%	_____	$ 57,200
TOTAL CLASS				$286,000

We know that 50 percent of the total sales was produced at a $25 price line; hence, $286,000 times 50 percent equals $143,000. This is how much you have to spend on the $25 price line. The same procedure is followed to determine the dollar purchases for the remaining price lines.

ASSORTMENT PLAN BY SIZE

FOR _____ CLASSIFICATION

VENDOR DISTRIBUTION   PERCENT TO TOTAL

_____   _____

_____   _____

_____   _____

_____   _____

_____   _____

_____   _____

_____   _____

_____   _____

_____   _____

                                       100%

JUSTIFICATION:

FIGURE 5.8   Perry's assortment plan by vendor

**PURCHASES BY CLASSIFICATION,
PERCENTAGE, AND DOLLARS**

CLASSIFICATION	PERCENT	✕ SEASON PURCHASES	= CLASS PURCHASES
_____	_____	_____	_____
_____	_____	_____	_____
_____	_____	_____	_____
_____	_____	_____	_____
_____	_____	_____	_____
_____	_____	_____	_____
_____	_____	_____	_____
_____	_____	_____	_____
_____	_____	_____	_____
_____	_____	_____	_____
_____	_____	_____	_____
TOTAL	**100%**		_____

FIGURE 5.9   Perry's purchases by classification, percentage, and dollars

To determine the number of units you can purchase, divide the price line dollars by the price line amount.

EXAMPLE:

50% of $286,000 = $\dfrac{\$143,000}{\$25 \text{ Price Line}}$ = 5,720 units to be purchased

Now the buyer knows approximately how many units at a $25 selling price will be needed to meet the yearly plan.

You should realize that a buyer's plans are comprehensive and help narrow the focus on the monumental task of spending exceedingly large sums of money.

Complete Figure 5.10 using plan purchases by classification to detail each classification by price line, units, and season-dollar totals. You will have to duplicate this page according to the number of classifications you have planned.

SIMULATION:
Go to Figure 5.10 in the book or Worksheet 17 on the CD-ROM.

PERRY'S

ASSORTMENT PLAN BY PRICE LINE, UNITS, AND DOLLARS

CLASSIFICATION	PRICE LINE	%	# OF UNITS	$ BY PRICE LINE	CLASS TOTAL
_____	_____	_____	_____	_____	
	_____	_____	_____	_____	
	_____	_____	_____	_____	$ _____
_____	_____	_____	_____	_____	
	_____	_____	_____	_____	
	_____	_____	_____	_____	$ _____
_____	_____	_____	_____	_____	
	_____	_____	_____	_____	
	_____	_____	_____	_____	$ _____
_____	_____	_____	_____	_____	
	_____	_____	_____	_____	
	_____	_____	_____	_____	$ _____

FIGURE 5.10   Perry's assortment plan by price line, units, and dollars

How to Shop the Market

* To prepare a six-month dollar merchandise plan
* The concept behind the 4-5-4 calendar
* To become confident in estimating plan figures
* To analyze last year's figures and competitive operating results
* To calculate open-to-buy

A buyer travels to market both to visit trade shows and to meet with individual vendors of merchandise that the buyer's store either carries or would like to consider carrying. The typical buyer of a small- to medium-size department store might travel to market or visit vendors anywhere from five to nine times a year. Employees from boutiques, specialty stores, and large department stores might visit more often, and most stores would have the vendor's representative visit their corporate headquarters or the location where the buyer works. The frequency of the market trips is based not only on the size of the organization but on the location and distance to the market, the department's target customer and his or her fashion innovation, and the structure and philosophy of the organization's management.

Depending on the location, the buyer may be in market for as little as one day or, if visiting foreign markets or overseas factories, the trip might extend beyond a week. The nature of the trip, whether it is to actually purchase merchandise or to seek out new trends and vendors or to develop product overseas, dictates the amount of time in market. The cost of market trips is significant; buyers today have limited resources and therefore must live within their travel budget. The cost-benefit of a market trip must be evaluated against the goals of that trip, and buyers must maximize their efforts to improve the profitability of their department. This requires buyers to pre-plan their market visits to make sure each trip is productive.

PRE-MARKET PLANNING

Timing of market trips is generally based on predetermined market dates that are set by each industry. For example, a men's wear buyer might go to one of many Web sites to determine which markets she would like to attend for each of her buying seasons. *Infomat* is a search engine for the fashion industry and provides market calendars based on apparel classifications, city, and month (http://www.infomat.com). Each listing also designates whether a show is for men's wear, women's wear, or children's wear and where it will be located. Further information on the Web site will also lead the buyer to the Web site of the trade show so that person can register and explore the organization of the show itself. Market Web sites traditionally inform the buyer of what classifications of merchandise will be shown, which vendors are renting booths at the show, and the actual floor plan of where the booths by number will be located. Additional information such as seminars, fashion shows, and other events may be listed as well as registration information.

SIMULATION:

Using the Infomat Web site, find a series of pages that lead you to the MAGIC (Men's Apparel Guild in California) Trade Show in Las Vegas occurring in February and August each year. The Web site www.magiconline.com will take you to the trade show Web site.

Explore the site and research the following information:

Date of the next market
Show floor categories
Show floor plans with booth numbers
List of seminars, fashion shows, and events

Present a report to your divisional merchandising manager (DMM) on the WWD MAGIC Trade Show and state the reasons why you should or should not attend this market.

RESEARCH BUSINESS STATISTICS

Approximately two weeks before the buyer travels to market to purchase merchandise, she reviews both her six-month dollar plan and the merchandise assortment plan, but she must also evaluate if the business goals from the previous season were met. The buyer should assess her performance by overall gross margin or maintained markup and also by classification and by vendor. This provides the buyer with information to review the performance of each vendor, to reassess each classification for viability and vitality, and to determine where growth and profitability for her department lies. The buyer will have a list of new vendors to visit, in addition to the performance of each major vendor in her department and a list of concerns to discuss with each vendor, including overall financial performance, shipping dates, order completion, order performance by styles or collections, and markdown money for those purchases that performed badly. More information on negotiating many of these issues will be discussed in Chapter 8.

Buying plans allow the buyer to examine present business conditions and project future performance for her department. A buyer reviews her plans to see how much money was spent for each period or month and how many units were purchased and delivered. With this information, the buyer projects forward to anticipate how much is on-hand (BOM stock) and how much should be ordered (Planned Purchases). To prepare for market, the buyer needs more specific information about what has sold and performed well and what merchandise has not met the profit goals for the department. Most department stores have numerous reports that support the research a buyer will need. Classification reports and unit sales reports will supply the buyer with information about trends by classification and by style. A vendor performance report will show profitability by each manufacturer. All of this data will help the buyer determine the strengths and weaknesses in last season's purchases, and analyze the current selling trends that will move into the next season.

In addition to the statistical information, the buyer needs to review promotional plans, special events, and the promotional calendar for the upcoming season to ensure that the right promotional merchandise is available for each month or event at the right price and in the right amount to meet consumer demand. With this research in hand, the buyer is ready to make appointments with vendors and shop the market.

PLANNING YOUR MARKET ITINERARY

There are many different ways to shop the market, and planning the itinerary depends on which market you attend and what type of merchandise you plan to buy. For example, if a buyer is shopping the New York City fashion market, which is organized primarily by building addresses within a three- to four-block radius, the buyer might shop by location or building to save time and to be more efficient. But if the buyer is shopping an apparel mart like Atlanta, she might decide to shop by classification. This allows her to keep color stories intact, critically shop each resource, and to take more fluid buying notes. Although this method requires more hours, a new buyer may find it helpful to think about only one classification at a time. For example, if the buyer is shopping for dresses for the junior department, she might spend a Tuesday afternoon at the Atlanta market meeting with only resources that sell dresses. At the end of the day, the buyer will review the notes she took at each vendor appointment as well as line lists or sketches. This narrowed vision might be less confusing and improve buying decisions compared to shopping many different classifications at the same time.

The third way to shop the market is to organize appointments by price points or price zones such as budget, moderate, or designer. Apparel markets or buying organizations often group manufacturers by similar customer base. Designer merchandise may be located in specific buildings in New York City or on a specific area of the layout or floor plan at MAGIC at the Las Vegas Convention Center or the AmericasMart in Atlanta.

Regardless of which way the buyer decides to shop the market, she sets appointments with her most important resources (vendors) based on sales volume and sell-through of units. This guarantees that these vendors have reserved enough time for the meeting, and the vendor can be prepared to discuss the store's account, sales, and any other issues both deem to be necessary. Appointments establish the buyer's priorities in market and ensure that each meeting will be productive. Buyers must also plan to seek out new resources, so time should be scheduled for "shopping new resources" and determining new trends. Buyers also "shop the competition" or other major retailers that are trendsetters or benchmarks for superior retailing. For example, a buyer in the New York City market would shop all the major department stores, visit select boutiques with a similar customer base, and observe people and their dress and lifestyle.

GETTING ORGANIZED

The buyer must organize a significant amount of information before going to market. First, she must bring her resource list with all of the pertinent contact information for each vendor. The buyer's file should include resource name, address, and phone number; manufacturer's representative's name, address, and phone number; and the names of each vendor's principals or leaders. These should be organized both alphabetically and by showroom address. This helps the buyer be efficient while in the market.

For each resource the buyer plans to visit, there should be a dollar volume report, a list of problems or issues with that vendor, special notes about each vendor, and special requests or actions the buyer wants to ask of that vendor. During a typical appointment the two might discuss the past season's sales, best sellers, worst sellers, future special promotions, markdown money to support lost margins, co-op advertising dollars, and a review of the upcoming line or collection. A good buyer also understands that strong relationships with vendors are essential to her success and might discuss more personal aspects of the sales representative's life, such as vacations, family, and hobbies before starting the business discussion of the meeting.

The buyer sets the tone of the meeting and must ensure that her agenda is at the forefront, not allowing the salesperson to dominate the meeting. This requires that the buyer be organized, articulate, and knowledgeable about her business with each vendor and what she needs from that vendor to be successful in the future. It is important that each buyer meet the principals of the company, who are often the ultimate decision makers. Developing a healthy rapport and sense of cooperation with the personnel of a company is essential; it is unprofessional to allow personal feelings for a manufacturer's salesperson to get in the way of doing business with that organization.

RESIDENT BUYING OFFICES

A good buyer is always searching for new trends that will produce a strong sell-through with excellent margins for her department. The first stop in market is often at a resident buying office, which provides buyers with market and fashion trend advice as well as many other services. Resident buying offices are usually located in a major apparel markets and are staffed with many specialists in various categories, including apparel, accessories, and home furnishings. Stores pay a fee for the services of the resident buying office, which can vary greatly, depending on the size of the store, the size and location of the buying offices, and the services that are provided.

Some of the services a resident buying office might provide for the buyer are:

* Reports on market and fashion trends

* Assistance with six-month dollar and merchandise assortment plans

* Introduction to new resources

* Group and import purchases

* Exclusivity of merchandise (private label and special purchases)

* Arrangement of vendor appointments

A resident buying office represents only noncompeting stores, so there is no conflict of interest in providing information to its clients (i.e., stores). There are other types of buying offices, and some large department stores have their own buying offices to assist buyers from the many different divisions and trading areas. Obviously, a buying office can save a buyer both time and money.

Most buying offices hold meetings during each major market for their stores. Additional meetings may be scheduled to plan import purchases. Meetings are generally held at the beginning of the week to familiarize buyers and merchandise managers with industry trends and styling prior to their shopping the market. Some buying offices have their meetings over a weekend, whereas others schedule meetings early in the workweek.

DISCOVERING TRENDS IN THE MARKET

There are many sources of trend information, and a buyer needs to be alert to the information that is spreading through the market. Listening to other buyers (even those from other stores) and manufacturer's sales representatives as well as shopping the stores will give the buyer many clues about what's hot in the fashion world. Each buyer must determine if the trend is right for her customer and if she wants to test an item to see how her customer might respond. The buyer must decide how much should be purchased in order to make an impact, which stores should carry the merchandise, and how many open-to-buy dollars it would it require. Remember that trends not only include styles but also may include color, fabrication, and lifestyle items. The buyer must also be aware of the basic or classic merchandise needs of her consumer, and plan for goods that sell season to season regardless of trends.

Experience will help a buyer determine the reliability of her sources. Over time, a buyer discovers the most accurate and useful sources of information about the market and trends. Each buyer must make her own decisions and not be pressured into buying something that is not right for her customer. She must also know what information she should and should *not* share in the marketplace. For example, a buyer should never brag about special favors or deals granted by a vendor, and she should avoid talking about her store's problems or personality conflicts among the employees.

MARKET ASSESSMENT AND DECISION MAKING

At the end of each day in market, the buyer should review her notes from the many different appointments and what she has seen during that day. She should sort her information by classification, delivery dates, price points, and trend. This allows the buyer to eliminate those items that are not preferred or are a duplication of another, more desirable item. For example, if shopping for women's black pants, a buyer might see 15 different styles and fabrications, but she must also keep in mind how many black pants actually are needed in that department. The buyer may decide on 5 styles and then pick the best of the 15 styles, filing away the information on the other 10 styles in case one of the first styles is unavailable.

The buyer determines desirability by determining if the merchandise is "on trend," at the right price, the right quality, and available when needed. Apparel buyers must consider the right "fit" for their customer, and all buyers must consider the item's selling record if previously purchased. Manufacturers can entice the buyer by offering advertising money, exclusivity, markdown allowances or guaranteed gross margin, terms and shipping allowances, and/or off-price merchandise.

With all of this information in mind, the buyer must eliminate merchandise from her "want" list in order to fit the open-to-buy. The buyer must then consider her sales floor and its physical appearance. How will she merchandise the purchases on the sales floor? Will the items hang together as a collection or be dispersed throughout the department? How many t-stands are in each department? Rounders? Waterfalls? A buyer also must think about units in addition to dollars. When viewing a new seasonal line, the buyer often will ask for a "style out" with the manufacturer's sales representative; this is when the buyer places the merchandise under consideration on a separate sales display rack to determine how the selected merchandise would look on the sales floor.

Most department store buyers do not write an order—or what is commonly called "drop paper"—when they are actually viewing a line of merchandise. They usually review their appointments, including their notes and line sheets, and then determine what they plan to buy after returning to their home office, where they write their purchase orders on the store's standard purchase order form. Usually, their boss, the DMM, must approve all the orders.

It is important for the buyer to be prepared for this meeting with her DMM. She should arrange the purchase orders progressively from most to least important, and should be able to explain how the purchases fit with the dollar plan and the assortment plan. The buyer must conceptualize what she wants to accomplish with her purchase. For instance, is the buyer trying to introduce new, trendy merchandise or merely "filling in the holes" of the basic merchandise assortment? Does the department want to expand in a certain classification or expand private label merchandise? The buyer has to make a case for, or defend, her purchases based on her departmental goals. One way she does this is to recap all of her orders by trends, dollars, and classification. She will use this information with the DMM and with store personnel to inform them of what has been purchased for their individual stores.

Divisional merchandise managers do not automatically approve all orders that a buyer presents. Because they are considering a bigger picture, the managers will ask many questions regarding assortment, gross margins, and the negotiation process to improve the buyer's business. Should a DMM not approve an order, the buyer can return later and reintroduce the items if the department's business or the market has changed.

DEVELOPING KEY RESOURCES

It is the buyer's responsibility to develop key resources that will contribute to and improve the department's business goals. Key resources make the buyer a "bigger fish" in a very competitive market. The success of the department then becomes more important to that vendor, which encourages a team mentality or partnership between the buyer and the vendor. Key resources need to understand how they fit into the financial plans and goals of the buyer's department, and what the buyer expects from the relationship. Some of the extras that a key resource might provide are exclusivity, shipping, advertising dollars, markdown allowances, guaranteed gross margin, off-price merchandise, and special promotions to coincide with major store sales or new store openings.

THE BUYER'S ROLE IN MARKET

The buyer represents her department and store at all times. This is especially important while in market. It is essential that she meet vendors on a regular basis, and if she is a new buyer, she should meet all of the vendors and be receptive to any complaints or problems. A buyer wants to develop a reputation as professional, responsive, and fair. Although the fashion industry is huge, the marketplace is relatively small when it comes to the reputations of its members. No buyer wants to be pegged as "unprofessional" or to "burn any bridges" that might limit their career aspirations or advancement in the future.

It is also imperative that a buyer knows store policy with regard to accepting gifts or even a vendor buying her a meal. News of impropriety spreads quickly in the marketplace and accepting a gift may could put the buyer's job in jeopardy. Buyers are expected to dress and act professionally while on market trips and should maintain a professional demeanor in all social situations.

SIMULATION:

Choose three new vendors you would like to visit on your next trip to market. Develop a profile of each vendor to present to your DMM, explaining why you would like to carry that specific line in your department. Compare that vendor with your customer profile.

The information in your new vendor report should include:

Company name and parent company (if applicable)
Address of sales office and manufacturer's sales representatives
Principals of company
Markets where company shows its merchandise
Product line description, including classifications and price points
Store(s) (A, B, or C) where this merchandise would be carried
Whether competitors of Perry's carry this merchandise
Whether this merchandise fills a void in Perry's assortment or is a replacement
  for another vendor's products

CHAPTER 7

STEP FIVE

Plan Market Purchases

IN THIS CHAPTER, YOU WILL LEARN:

* The steps to plan a market trip itinerary
* The major market weeks
* The merchandise selection process
* To write purchase orders and compare terms of the sale
* To understand the flow of merchandise to the sales floor

Market trips are planned by the buyer primarily to purchase merchandise for each season. Other reasons for visiting the *market* include building vendor relationships and negotiating with *resources*. Buyers generally plan the number of market trips to be taken according to market dates, store and customer needs, and proximity of the store's location to the market.

PREPLANNING

Prior to scheduling a market trip for the opening of a season, detailed plans must be finalized and approved by the *divisional merchandise manager (DMM)* and *general merchandise manager (GMM)*. A six-month dollar plan should be completed and a stock assortment strategy developed. The stock assortment plan determines relevant classifications, subclassifications, price points, units, colors, sizes, and fabrication. Trade magazines for your industry, such as *Earnshaw's, Women's Wear Daily* (*WWD*), and *Home Furnishings News* (*HFN*), should be perused, as these contain pertinent information on current market trends.

Now that you have executed a six-month plan, concluded the stock assortment plan, and understand your responsibilities while at market, you are ready to schedule a market trip to either New York City or another market appropriate to your merchandise assortment.

Market trips generally last three to four days. Airline reservations are often coordinated by the DMM's secretary or company travel agent. A hotel room should be booked for this trip for two nights, allowing you three days in the market. All reservations should be secured as far in advance as possible, as vacancies fill rapidly during major market weeks.

The next task is to prepare an itinerary. Figure 7.1 is an example of an itinerary prepared by a children's wear buyer.

As reviewed in Chapter 6, suggested ways to shop the market are by vendor importance, classification, building, or price line. Because many vendors offer more than one classification of merchandise, the market will be shopped by resource, in order of importance.

SIMULATION:
Go to Figure 7.2 in the book or Worksheet 18 on the CD-ROM and to your department's catalogue and Industry Statistics on the CD-ROM.

Using the itinerary form in Figure 7.2, begin to schedule your market week appointments, contacting key vendors first. Be sure to include the company name, building and room number, telephone number, and sales representative's name on the itinerary. An itinerary will be left with the divisional secretary and distributed to the DMM, GMM, and other buyers in your division who will be traveling with you.

Refer to your CD-ROM for a resource list of key vendors for your industry. You should add additional resources of your choice. Keep in mind that the DMM typically spends time viewing major lines with each buyer in the division. On occasion, the GMM also accompanies the DMM. Therefore, be sure to confer with the DMM to select appointments so you can view the lines together.

Time should also be allotted for visiting local stores and the buying office to look for new vendors and merchandising ideas.

Major markets for women's ready-to-wear in New York City are traditionally held in January, March, May, August, and October. Transitional and Fall I are shopped in March, followed by Fall II in May. Holiday goods are available in August with spring merchandise offered in October. Summer apparel is at the market in January. In February and August, most men's wear buyers attend the ***Men's Apparel Guild in California (MAGIC)*** show in Las Vegas. The Atlanta International Gift and Home Furnishings show is the primary home fashions market with major shows each January and July. Market dates may shift due to calendar changes and unexpected events.

From your buying office representative, or a trend-forecasting source, you will

PERRY'S

BUYER K. Videtic   **HOTEL** Hotel Metro

DEPT. 110 Infants   **PHONE** 212-555-1212

	MONDAY	TUESDAY	WEDNESDAY	THURSDAY	FRIDAY
8:00	Buying office				
8:30	Buying office				
9:00	Buying office	**Baby Dove**	**Baby Buns**	**Quiltex Marty**	
9:30	Buying office	112 W. 34th R: 1111	112 W. 34th R: 1610	(at buying office)	
10:00	**Carters**	564-1713 Jan	695-2225 Joseph		
10:30	100 W. 33rd R: 1125	**Buster Brown**	**Ester Burnstein**	**Healthtex**	
11:00	868-1600 Leo	112 W. 34th R: 1000	112 W. 34th R: 2211	112 W. 34th R: 2201	
11:30		947-7980 Don	279-1141 Ester	502-6000	
12:00	**Official School Unif.**			**Leave for Airport**	
12:30	100 W. 33rd R: 1012	**Haddad Bros**	**Baby Togs**		
1:00	502-6000 Jared	112 W. 34th R: 1555	112 W. 34th R: 1112		
1:30		563-2117 Mel	868-2100 Sam		
2:00	**Esprit Kids**	**Baby Town**			
2:30	100 W. 33rd R: 1007	112 W. 34th R: 1505	**Sweet Potatoes**		
3:00	594-5511 John	239-1112 Susan	34 W. 34th R: 2701		
3:30	**Baby Town**	**Sage Creek**	239-4060		
4:00	112 W. 34th R:	112 W. 34th R: 1104	**Peaches and Cream**		
4:30	239-1112	239-4660 Janice	34 W. 34th R: 2709		
5:00	**Shop Retailers**	**Gund**	239-4660		
5:30		112 W. 34th R: 1012			
		279-4863			

FIGURE 7.1   Sample Perry's travel itinerary

PERRY'S

BUYER

DEPT.

HOTEL

PHONE

	MONDAY	TUESDAY	WEDNESDAY	THURSDAY	FRIDAY
8:00					
8:30					
9:00					
9:30					
10:00					
10:30					
11:00					
11:30					
12:00					
12:30					
1:00					
1:30					
2:00					
2:30					
3:00					
3:30					
4:00					
4:30					
5:00					
5:30					

FIGURE 7.2   Perry's travel itinerary

receive a market-planning guide that recaps important topics covered during the market meeting (discussed in Chapter 6). The planning guide contains an overview of the market, fashion direction in color, fabrication, and styling along with a suggested resource structure. In addition to attending the market week meeting, schedule a separate appointment to meet with the buying office representative for your area to discuss Perry's needs. After conversing with the buying office representative, you are ready to shop the market.

You can find an example of a fall report from a resident buying office forecaster on your CD-ROM.

Using the following outline and previous research, prepare a fashion office report for the current fall season.

SIMULATION: *Go to the fall market trend report on the CD-ROM.*

> **I.** Overview
>
> **II.** Fashion Direction
> > **A.** Colors
> > **B.** Prints and Patterns
> > **C.** Fabrications
> > **D.** Silhouettes
>
> **III.** Classifications
> > (highlight key information for each important classification)
>
> **IV.** Market/Economic Trends
>
> **V.** Impact of Trends on Your Industry

VISITING RESOURCES

When buyers begin shopping a line, vendors often provide catalogues with pictures or line lists to facilitate the selection process. Each item is given a style number that indicates to the manufacturer the particular season, silhouette, and fabric.

Merchandise is shown either by groupings or by items. While examining the merchandise, it is important to consider the price, styling, color, fabrication, and quality. First, determine what retail price will sell the merchandise and then compare that to the actual cost. If the markup achieved is acceptable, then the item is worth the cost.

Second, select styles reflective of the customer's needs rather than your own personal taste. It is of utmost importance to remember that it is the customer who will ultimately purchase the merchandise.

To make the selection process easier, eliminate the styles that do not meet your requirements. From the remaining selection, rank the styles in order of preference. Buyers use various systems of ranking, such as 1, 2, 3, or single, double, and triple asterisks, or check marks. Select a system that works well for you.

The vendor's *sales representative* can also provide guidance in decision-making by noting top-booking numbers or projected best-sellers. Many resources utilize road representatives who can even better indicate the most appropriate styles for a particular territory.

Once the initial numbers have been chosen, ask the vendor to do a *style out* by placing together all numbers selected. Make final eliminations if there is any duplication or overlap. It is much easier to narrow the line while in the showroom than to wait until later, when it is more difficult to remember styling details.

The final step is to negotiate prices and terms with the vendor. Terms of the sale are discussed later in this chapter as a separate topic; negotiation skills ae reviewed in Chapter 8.

WRITING PURCHASE ORDERS

Prior to writing purchase orders, review and analyze the lines at the end of the market trip to recheck for duplication and to determine the resources most advantageous to fill the needs of the store. For this reason, it is not advisable to leave orders or " *drop paper*" while shopping the market—wait until returning to the store to finalize orders.

Some vendors request *bulk estimates* of quantities while the buyer is in the market. If you comply with this request, emphasize that a bulk estimate is *not* a confirmed quantity.

After careful selection of styles, a breakdown or distribution of quantities by vendor, color, size, and store should be allocated on a worksheet. The order worksheets should be totaled by cost and retail to determine the markup as well as to compare plan dollars and units to th previous year's figures. When you are satisfied with the order, transfer the information to an order form. Many larger stores now transmit orders via *electronic data interchange (EDI)*.

Most stores use their own order forms for uniformity. A sample order form (purchase order) from Perry's Department Store is shown in Figure 7.3. The retail store usually lists the conditions of the purchase on the back of the order form. Stores that do not have their own order forms use order forms provided by the vendor.

It is important to fill in all information accurately and legibly so mistakes will not be made in calculating and filling the order. At Perry's, a prenumbered order form consists of four copies. One copy is distributed to the vendor, another to the store accounts payable, another to the store warehouse, and another to the buyer. Typical information needed to complete the order form is as follows:

Date of order
Department number
Vendor name and address
Vendor number (assigned by the store)
FOB point
Shipping instructions/routing
Terms of sale
Delivery/cancel dates
Style number
Classification number
Description of merchandise
Colors
Sizes
Quantity ordered
Unit cost
Total cost dollars
Unit retail
Total retail dollars
Markup percent
Buyer/DMM/GMM signatures
Special instructions

Using the vendor catalogue found on the CD-ROM for your department, select styles and write one order on Figure 6.3. Use the order above as a guide in completing the order form. Be sure to review styles to eliminate duplication. For apparel, spend from $5,000 to $10,000 for one delivery period. For home fashion/giftware, spend from $2,000 to $4,000 for one delivery period. Distribute merchandise to all stores based on customer profile and store ranking. Be sure to research the market or apparel mart to plan for the correct week and to make sure that your key vendors are attending the show you plan to attend.

SIMULATION: *Go to Figure 7.3 in the book or Worksheet 19 on the CD-ROM and to your department's catalogue on the CD-ROM.*

DELIVERY DATES

When planning for delivery of merchandise, vendors will quote a delivery date consisting of a start ship date and a cancellation date. To further clarify the cancellation date, the store designates whether the merchandise is to be "shipped by" or "in store" by the cancellation date. For example, 8/1–8/25 "shipped by" cancellation means that goods can be shipped to the store beginning August 1, but can be shipped no later than August 25. Perry's uses a cancellation date that states "shipped by."

When the buyer purchases goods from the vendor, the means of transportation to the store must be decided. The transportation cost is part of the cost of the merchandise, and therefore careful consideration should be given to the means of delivery. Delivery terms will determine at what point ownership of the merchandise passes from the vendor to the store

TERMS OF THE SALE

Because the buyer purchases inventory to sell at a profit for the company, the vendor's *terms of the sale* must be examined closely. The terms of the sale encompass discounts on the quoted price of merchandise, the timing of the payment, and the guidelines for transportation.

Vendors allow certain types of discounts to be taken on merchandise offered for sale. These reductions should be negotiated prior to confirming an order. Types of discounts include quantity discounts, seasonal discounts, trade discounts, and cash discounts. Discounts lower the cost of the goods, which, in turn, causes gross margin to increase.

Quantity discounts are extended to a buyer for ordering a large sum of merchandise. The discount is quoted as a percentage off. For example, an item that sells at a line price of $20 might be reduced to $15, a 25 percent discount, if at least 600 units are ordered.

Seasonal discounts are offered on merchandise bought prior to the normal buying season. For example, if orders are placed for outerwear jackets 12 months in advance of the selling season, a reduced percentage (perhaps 15 percent) may be given by the vendor. This may also be called *incentive purchasing*.

Trade discounts are a percentage or percentages deducted from the retail list price of merchandise. An example is sterling silver flatware. The vendor establishes the suggested retail price and offers the buyer a trade discount off the list price. If the list price of a sterling silver baby spoon is $95 and the buyer is given a trade discount of 50 percent, the cost of the spoon would be $47.50.

PURCHASE ORDER

Name		**Perry's Department Store**	PO #	01971
Address		**15203 King Street**	Dept. #	
City		**Fredericksburg, VA 22401**	Vendor #	
State/ZIP			DUNS #	

FOB _____

This order is subject to the terms and conditions on the reverse side of this sheet.	**TRANSPORTATION**	With anticipation for prepayment all dating except EOM begins at date merchandise is received. Under EOM terms all goods shipped on and received after the 25th of the month are to be dated as of the first of the following month.	Start ship _____
	Vendor _____ %		Cancel _____
	Store _____ %		Terms _____
	Allowance $ _____		Page ____ of ____
	Ship Via _____		

DESCRIPTION	CL	STYLE	COLOR	DWNT	DALE	CARO	STAF	SPOT	QUANTITY	COST UNIT	COST TOT	RETAIL UNIT	RETAIL TOT

Special Instructions

Buyer Signature _____ Date _____

DMM/GMM _____ Date _____

MU%

INVOICE INSTRUCTIONS
Submit separate invoice for each store. Show order and department number on each invoice. Invoice must accompany shipment in an envelope attached to the lead carton marked Invoice Enclosed.

PACKING AND SHIPPING
Pack merchandise separately for each store with individual packing slips. Mark each carton with the store name, order number, department number, and number of cartons in shipment. Ship complete unless otherwise instructed.

FIGURE 7.3 Perry's purchase order form

Cash discounts are a percentage of deduction taken for paying an invoice within the specified time allowed. The discount motivates the purchaser to pay invoices on time. A common example of apparel terms is 8/10 EOM. If the invoice is paid within 10 days after the end of the month, an 8 percent discount may be deducted from the bill. If the payment is not made by the designated time allowed, the full amount of the invoice must be remitted with no discount deduction.

The amount of time allowed for payment of an invoice is referred to as *dating*. Types of dating include regular dating, EOM dating, extra dating, and receipt of goods (ROG) dating.

In *regular dating*, the cash discount and net periods are figured from the date of the invoice. An invoice date of September 5 and terms of 8 percent–10 days, net 30, would allow an 8 percent discount if payment is made by September 15. If the payment is made 11 to 30 days from the date of invoice, no discount is allowed and the full, or net, amount is due. Payment made after 30 days is considered past due.

EOM dating is computed from the end of the month. Using 8/10 EOM as an example, an invoice dated October 10, with payment made by November 10, would receive an 8 percent discount. An exception to this is an invoice dated on or after the 25th of the month. These invoices are handled as if the invoice date was the beginning of the following month. Therefore, an invoice dated November 25, with EOM terms, would be due by January 10 in order to receive the 8 percent discount. Although not specified in the terms, it is understood that there is a 30-day net payment period from the end of the month before considering the invoice past due. Using the preceding example, an invoice dated November 25, with 8/10 EOM terms, paid on January 30, would not be past due, but the 8 percent discount would no longer be allowed.

Extra dating may be negotiated to allow a longer period of time to pay the invoice and still receive a discount. Extra dating is often requested for seasonal goods delivered early or for new store openings. For example, 2/10 + 30 indicates that an extra 30 days are permitted before payment, along with a 2 percent discount. Extra dating is typically listed in 30-day increments, such as 30, 60, 90 days, or beyond.

Receipt of goods (ROG) dating stands for dating as of receipt of goods. Rather than calculating the discount period from the date of invoice, the date the merchandise is delivered to the store is used to determine the payment period. ROG dating is used when the delivery period may be longer than usual because of a greater distance between the vendor and retailer. With ROG dating, the retailer avoids paying for merchandise before it has been delivered to the store and placed on the selling floor.

TRANSPORTATION

The retailer absorbs a major portion of the transportation cost. Therefore, the buyer must carefully plan the routing of goods from the FOB point.

The *FOB point* is the location where the merchandise changes ownership from manufacturer to store. FOB stands for "free on board." The most widely used term is *FOB factory*, which means that the store takes ownership of the merchandise once the goods leave the factory of the manufacturer. In other words, the store is responsible for all of the freight charges plus insurance. *FOB store* means that the manufacturer pays all freight charges and insurance; this is a cost savings to the store. The buyer designates the shipper to be used for transportation. United Parcel Service (UPS) is often used for shipments of less than 50 pounds. Trucking companies are a cost-effective means of transportation, with a delivery time of three to five days, depending on the distance to the store. Air freight is the most expensive method of transportation, but it is often used when shipping merchandise from coast to coast or for deliveries needed in one or two days. The buyer must consider both the expense of transportation and the time frame for delivery.

BUYING CALENDAR AND MERCHANDISE FLOW

A buying calendar for apparel has been provided in Figure 7.4 to illustrate how seasonal purchases and delivery dates are designated by market.

Use the buying calendar as a guideline when planning purchases. In addition, import items are ordered through the resident buying office 6 to 12 months in advance of the fall/holiday and spring/summer seasons. A reserve fund of 5 to 10 percent of open-to-buy should be kept for immediate purchases of "hot" items, reorders, and off-price merchandise.

In some industries, certain basic styles are in constant demand by the consumer. Perry's, as so many other stores, implements an automatic reorder system to maintain a "never out" stock status on staple items. Best-selling styles continue to reorder, changing fabrication by season. Fashion items, depending on the individual item, are on a 6- to 12-week cycle before markdown.

APPAREL BUYING CALENDAR AND MERCHANDISE FLOW

MONTH	MARKET	DELIVERY	EVENTS
January	Summer	March April May	Vacation
March	Transitional Early Fall	June July	Back-to-School
May	Fall	August September	Holiday Catalogues Fall/Holiday Promotions
August	Holiday Cruise Early Spring	October November December January	After-Christmas Promotions
October	Spring	January February	Easter

FIGURE 7.4   Perry's buying calendar

CHAPTER 8

Negotiating Profitability

IN THIS CHAPTER, YOU WILL LEARN:

* The fundamental steps of effective negotiation
* How to recognize different styles of negotiation
* Several points to review to assist in negotiating in retail buying
* The importance of cross-cultural negotiation

Negotiation is part of our daily lives, used when we want to persuade someone to do something or to obtain something for ourselves. We negotiate with our families, our friends, our coworkers, and just about everyone we come in contact with. In order to be an effective negotiator, it is important for buyers to first learn the fundamentals of negotiation.

NEGOTIATION PREPARATION

The most important part of the negotiation process is preparation. The first step in negotiating is to gather all relevant information and analyze the situation. For a retail buyer this means you must learn as much as possible about the vendor's side or per-spective (imagine yourself as the vendor's sales representative in order to gain that person's insight) and identify the related business issues as well as your own departmental issues. Some of the information you might collect would include an assessment or evaluation of the vendor's performance for your department, the markdowns in dollars of that specific merchandise, or percentage of your total dollar purchases from that merchandise. With these facts, you could determine who has the advantage: the buyer or the vendor. For example, if a buyer is considering a purchase from a vendor, does the vendor need the buyer's business? Or does the vendor have highly desired merchandise that the buyer needs? In the first situation, if the vendor needs the buyer's business, the buyer has the advantage. On the other hand, if the vendor has a brand name of merchandise that is in great demand by the buyer, the vendor has the advantage. Having the advantage means more negotiating power, and negotiating power improves the possibility of getting a desired outcome. For a retail buyer, that desired outcome would mean a better price or improved profitability.

RELATIONSHIP POWER

If the buyer has a strong relationship with a vendor, the power to negotiate is increased. A buyer who establishes rapport with a vendor will usually have a relationship style that is more cooperative than competitive. Buyers should see beyond the individual purchase and consider their affiliation with a vendor as a long-term association that creates prosperity and success for both retailer and manufacturer. The relationship between buyer and vendor should be considered a partnership that creates win-win opportunities.

As with any working friendship, there are many different ways to promote the relationship between buyer and vendor. Vendors remember birthdays and holidays and, of course, buyers should do the same. Buyers can also improve their standing with a specific vendor by developing strategies that will increase sales for both. A buyer might develop special promotional plans with a specific vendor, such as in-store events like trunk shows or special giveaways. Another method a buyer can use to create a stronger relationship with a vendor is to place significant orders. The higher the volume of purchases, the more important a buyer is to the supplier. A good buyer will build volume with fewer suppliers to create relationship power. Remember that relationship power creates negotiating power.

As a part of a buyer's preparation, she must consider the needs of the supplier to discover where there is room to negotiate. If the vendor has already given markdown money, there is less room in other areas to negotiate. The vendor usually grants markdown money based on a percentage of the retail purchases. The buyer should find out the expectations of the vendor and anticipate possible objections. After reviewing vendor performance and previous business arrangements, the buyer determines what she wants their negotiations to accomplish and sets objectives to achieve that goal. For example, does the buyer want a lower price or does she want the vendor to pay for shipping? A strong negotiating plan includes opening, middle, and closing strategies. Good negotiators are flexible. A good buyer develops alternative strategies to cover all angles after presenting the initial offer. The buyer asks for what is needed to achieve departmental financial goals, while also understanding that a few concessions may be necessary to complete the business negotiation. A fair business transaction is generally a compromise somewhere in the mid range of what both parties are seeking. The best scenario is to have a win-win outcome where both parties get what they want and are satisfied.

NEGOTIATION MEETING

After the buyer prepares for negotiation and develops a plan or an agenda, the next step is to meet with the vendor. Determine who the leader and decision makers are so time is not wasted negotiating with someone who is not in the position to make a decision. A vendor's salesperson is often unable to negotiate buying terms, and the company's sales manager or owner (sometimes known as the "principals") must be included in the discussion. For best results, negotiate in person rather than by phone or e-mail, and, if possible, keep negotiations between just two people. When additional parties are involved, there will be more discussion and opinions to be heard, resulting in a greater length of time before decisions can be made.

As the buyer begins the meeting, she must first build the relationship with the vendor and set the tone of the meeting. It is important that the buyer remain in charge and not let the vendor take control of the situation. When the buyer takes control of the meeting, it is then an appropriate time to present the offer or the problem or information in a clear and concise manner. The buyer should go through her agenda, making sure to cover all of her points. She should state her requests and support them with facts. The more information and supporting facts a buyer has, the more likely she will be to achieve a positive result. Remember to quantify information for a more powerful negotiating position: a "15 percent decrease in sales" is a more powerful statement than "sales are down." If the buyer is negotiating to resolve a problem, and the initial response of the vendor is not what is desired, solicit assistance from the vendor. The buyer should ask the vendor for suggestions to help arrive at a solution that is acceptable to both.

A buyer's meeting agenda might look like this:

1. Thank vendor for that person's support over the last quarter.

2. Review top three sellers of the vendor's line and each item's sell-through.

3. Discuss late shipments and broken assortments for March and April.

4. Ask for RTVs (returns to vendor) for broken assortments, and markdown dollars for lost revenue due to late shipments and broken assortments.

5. Discuss next market purchases with regard to terms and as a percentage of department's total volume.

Negotiations can be cooperative or competitive. Cooperative negotiation is most likely to result in a win-win situation. The interests and needs of both sides must be met for the negotiation to be effective. A good negotiator knows it is important to listen to the needs of the other person, allowing him or her to speak without interruption. The buyer should respond with questions for clarification and summarize what has been said to acknowledge that the vendor's needs have been heard. The buyer should be ready to offer an alternate choice, or concession if the negotiation hits a snag. Planning ahead of time about how to address a negative response will give the buyer more negotiating power. A cooperative negotiator exercises patience, listens carefully, and is open to compromise. A competitive negotiator who "plays tough" and uses intimidation to achieve desired goals may succeed, but only creates a win-lose situation. It is therefore better to use persuasion than intimidation.

CLOSING THE NEGOTIATIONS

While planning for the negotiation meeting, prepare a checklist of points to review at the end of the meeting so that nothing important is overlooked. Repeat back to the vendor what has been agreed upon and how it will take place (including the time frame and any other details pertinent to the agreement). Assess the appropriate amount of time needed to close the negotiation and reach an agreement. Rushing to complete the negotiation can be as ineffective as taking too long to conclude. Be sure to document the agreement in writing, and preferably have both parties sign and date the agreement.

A checklist or closing review might look like this:

Points to Review

1. Discuss late shipments and broken assortments in March and April

2. Review percentage of total merchandise that is invested with vendor

3. Review sell-through on March/April shipments and lost revenues

4. Ask for return of broken assortments sent in March and April

5. Ask for discount of new merchandise to counter lost revenue

6. Discuss chargebacks for RTVs

NEGOTIATION OF PURCHASES

There are many opportunities for the retail buyer to use negotiation skills. A buyer begins a season with negotiating terms of sale for purchases and ends the season with negotiating profit margin based on sales performance. Terms of sale to negotiate include:

* Payment terms

* Freight charges

* Price and discounts

* Allowances (markdowns, advertising, fixtures, signage, etc.)

NEGOTIATION PAYMENT TERMS

When the buyer views merchandise from a vendor, the vendor informs the buyer of the general payment terms offered by the company. The terms, referred to as dating, define the amount of time allowed before paying the invoice. Buyers often negotiate for extra dating, which is additional time past regular terms to pay the invoice. If a vendor is promoting a new product but the buyer is hesitant to purchase the item, the buyer may ask for an additional 30 or 60 days' dating to try the product.

Suppliers may also offer dating programs for placing orders early for seasonal goods. In the home fashion market, vendors will introduce Christmas merchandise in January. Because buyers do not take delivery of items until July or later, and may want to wait until closer to the time of need before placing an order, some vendors may offer dating as of December 1 for a limited time to entice buyers to place orders early. This means instead of net 30 terms, a buyer could have Christmas merchandise on the selling floor for almost the entire season before paying the invoice on December 1. The benefit to the vendor is that best-selling items are identified earlier, allowing time to adjust production to more accurately anticipate sales.

Another common request for extra dating is when a new store opens. When a department store opens another location, a buyer will typically request additional dating for orders placed for the new store. Obviously, merchandise for the new store must arrive early enough to allow sufficient time to set the selling floor before the store's grand opening. Because the merchandise will not be available for immediate sales when it is received, the additional time before paying the invoice helps the retailer's cash flow situation. See Chapter 6 for more information on types of dating.

NEGOTIATING FREIGHT CHARGES

The retail store is generally responsible for paying freight on all incoming shipments once each leaves the factory. Orders with such terms are *FOB factory*. Sometimes buyers will negotiate for the freight to be paid by the vendor, or *FOB store*. This is a cost savings to the buyer, as freight charges can be significant. The further a vendor is located from the retail store, the higher the freight charges will be. A buyer from a store located in California will often ask for a freight cap if the vendor is shipping from the East Coast. In this case, an agreed-upon percentage of the net total of merchandise is the maximum the buyer will pay. For example, a buyer may request that freight charges not exceed 5 percent of the total net cost of the merchandise. If the freight charges actually total 7 percent, the supplier will absorb the remaining 2 percent. If a vendor wants the order from the buyer, this may be a concession to do business.

NEGOTIATING PRICE AND DISCOUNTS

There are several types of discounts a buyer can negotiate to reduce the quoted price of merchandise. Two of the most common are quantity and seasonal discounts. Buyers who place a high volume of orders may request a discount based on purchasing a large quantity of units. It is assumed that the greater the number of units ordered, the more cost-effective it is for the vendor to produce and ship the merchandise. A vendor would much rather make a sale of 3,000 units to one buyer than sales of 100 units to 30 buyers. The percentage of discount will vary depending on the volume of goods purchased. A buyer may also negotiate a discount based on total dollar volume purchased from a vendor. For example, a buyer may promise the supplier a substantial increase of business over the previous year if the vendor will sell a specified amount of goods at 25 percent off on an order placed at the start of the season. Or, if the volume is high enough and the store important enough to the vendor, the buyer may demand a certain percentage off all merchandise purchased.

Buyers also seek off-price opportunities from vendors. Merchandise that a vendor is closing out can be product that has not sold well, odds and ends that are left over, or discontinued merchandise. *Closeouts* are offered at a discount that is greater than the usual percentage. There may be a limited quantity of each item, so suppliers may prefer to sell an assortment of many different styles rather than allowing the buyer to select individual styles of merchandise. It is better to try to select merchandise in order to avoid purchasing unwanted styles that might not sell. Generally, assorted merchandise can be negotiated at a lower discount. Vendors may not offer off-price merchandise, leaving it up to the buyer to ask about what is available.

Seasonal discounts may apply for merchandise ordered in advance of a season. A vendor who sells Christmas merchandise may give a percentage off regular wholesale cost to all customers who make an early buy. In this case, to qualify, a predetermined minimum dollar amount must be purchased as early as January, but may not be shipped until August.

In the gift industry, vendors often give a case pack discount to all buyers who purchase in case pack increments rather than minimum quantity. If an item sells at a wholesale price of $10 for a minimum of four units, a vendor may offer a discount of 5 percent or more if the buyer will purchase the case pack of 24 units.

NEGOTIATING ALLOWANCES

Buyer negotiation for allowances is ongoing throughout the year. In the beginning of the year, new store, shortage, and advertising allowances may be negotiated in a contract, although some stores may negotiate advertising on a per ad basis. Buying operations will often ask for a new store percentage allowance in lieu of requesting merchandise discounts each time a new store is opened. The buyer may also request an allowance for shortage based on the percentage of department shrinkage. Advertising allowance may be negotiated based on a percentage of net purchases from a vendor. If a vendor does not agree to provide an advertising allowance, a buyer may load the cost of an item and later, after the ad has run, charge the loaded amount back to the vendor as advertising allowance. This method is not favorable, because loading additional cost to the wholesale price of the item leads to an inflated and less competitive retail price.

Buyers should also discuss substitution, damages, exchange, and return policies with the vendor prior to ordering merchandise. It is best to note that no substitutions are to be made without approval from the buyer. Often a best-selling item may be sold out and a vendor may request to substitute another style. The other style may be less desirable or may not coordinate with the collection purchased. In a similar vein, if merchandise arrives damaged, most domestic vendors will allow the buyer to return the merchandise. For imported merchandise, it is not cost-effective to return damaged or poor-quality items. In this situation, the buyer should negotiate a deduction from the full price. Some retail operations negotiate a percentage of net sales up front for damage allowance, but will charge a vendor back for any damaged merchandise that exceeds the allowance. If the merchandise is damaged, the retailer charges the vendor the freight to return the goods. Often the vendor accepts the chargeback for the damaged product, but requests that the retailer dispose of the goods rather than the vendor having to pay freight to return merchandise that is no longer of use.

The most important goal of a buyer is to make a profit for the company. Buyers analyze selling reports to determine the success and profitability of merchandise, comparing actual sales, markdowns, turnover, and gross margin to plan. When merchandise is not selling as well as expected, the buyer may either ask to return the product or request markdown assistance. Vendors are reluctant to accept returned merchandise for several reasons. Because the product has been opened and placed in the store for sale and marked with the retailer's tag, the merchandise may not be as saleable to another company. Also, it will be difficult for the vendor to find another buyer to take the merchandise after the season has begun. As a compromise, a buyer may ask to exchange the product for additional merchandise of a different type or reorder merchandise that is selling well. The buyer may also request a dollar allowance, or markdown money, from the vendor to share the markdown and salvage the profit margin. It is best to ask for assistance with markdown money as soon as poor-selling merchandise is identified. A buyer has a better chance of receiving markdown assistance mid-season rather than waiting until the end of the season when most buyers review profitability.

If a markdown allowance is granted, the vendor usually prefers that the buyer deduct the amount from the next invoice rather than sending a check for the amount to the retailer. If the supplier invoice has already been paid and a buyer is not continuing to do business with the vendor, a debit balance will be created. The buyer will then need to try to persuade the vendor to write a check to the retailer, or will be forced to purchase additional merchandise to cover the amount of the debit. Sometimes a retailer will hold invoices from a new vendor in anticipation of any problems. Many buyers share selling reports with their suppliers on a regular basis to prevent possible surprises at the end of the season. Larger retail operations may negotiate a specific percentage of net sales up front to cover markdowns as part of an annual contract. Vendors are reluctant to accept this, but often will agree in order to maintain business with a desirable account. Buyers may also discuss expectations of gross margin, negotiating a specified guaranteed margin agreement.

CANCELLATIONS

When a purchase order is written, signed, and submitted to the vendor, it is considered a binding contract. However, there are certain conditions that may occur that lead a buyer to ask to cancel an order. When a department is overbought, management will ask the buyer for ways to reduce the stock level. A buyer will review selling history of merchandise and open orders to determine if there is any merchandise on order that should be cancelled. If a classification of merchandise is overbought or not performing well, the buyer may seek to cancel additional merchandise on order for the weak classification to bring the stock-to-sales ratio in line. There may also be a reorder placed for an item that is not selling as well as projected. In cases such as these, the buyer should gather selling results to present to the supplier in support of canceling the merchandise. Although facts support the cancellation, the supplier may have already produced the merchandise and may not be willing to let the buyer out of the contract. This is where negotiation skills and concessions come into play to create a win-win situation for both parties. The best scenario is that a buyer from another company needs that stock immediately and is willing to accept the order, but this is rarely the case. Perhaps the order can be moved to a future delivery date, giving the product a longer selling period to reduce stock. Of course, the buyer could always refuse the shipment when it is delivered, but this results in a win-lose situation that could strain the relationship. The buyer wins in reducing the stock, but the vendor loses when the merchandise is returned.

CROSS-CULTURAL NEGOTIATION

In today's global market, buyers must be prepared for cross-cultural negotiation. More buyers than ever are traveling widely to attend foreign trade shows and work with factories throughout Asia and other parts of the world, seeking a competitive advantage in pricing, uniqueness, or exclusivity. To negotiate effectively in the international business arena, it is crucial to understand the cultural differences and business etiquette of the country you desire to conduct business with. Often business deals fail due to the lack of understanding of values, beliefs, etiquette, and communication of a culture that differs from that of the negotiator. By accepting the fact that diverse cultures have different perspectives, the negotiator is less likely to view the situation in a negative manner.

Relevance of Time in Cross-Cultural Negotiation

There are distinct cultural differences when dealing with the perception of time. The two most commonly identified approaches to time management are known as monochronic and polychronic.

It is important to the *monochronic culture* to be punctual and to follow a schedule. Being late for a meeting would be considered disrespectful. Issues to be discussed are dealt with one at a time, in sequential order. This type of culture searches for facts to present specific information, with accurate details. Commitment is to the job, with less significance on relationships. Monochronic cultures include Germany, Scandinavia, Switzerland, the United States, and the United Kingdom. Negotiators in the United Kingdom sometimes use pressure strategies including setting definitive deadlines. Decisions may take a longer time in Germany.

Polychronic cultures are much more adaptable, but are easily distracted. They are inclined to already have the facts. Polychronic negotiators are comfortable dealing with multiple situations and people concurrently. In Japan, a team of negotiators may come to a decision by consensus. The polychronic are committed to long-term relationships. Schedules are flexible and punctuality is not important. Polychronic cultures will take as long as needed to complete the negotiation, not allowing a schedule to dictate timing. This type of arrangement is more prevalent in Africa, France, Greece, Italy, and Mexico.

Personal Space

One aspect of personal space refers to the distance between people and whether or not they feel comfortable being touched. In China, Europe, Japan, and North America, many people like to have a space of two to four feet between themselves and the other party. They may also prefer not to be touched by those they do not know or feel comfortable with. But Arab, Latin America, and Mediterranean cultures find touching acceptable. Another consideration of space is associated with eye contact. In Arab and North American cultures, eye contact indicates truthfulness and reliability. Direct eye contact also conveys confidence. However, in other cultures, such as Japan, direct eye contact is considered rude and therefore avoided. Similarly, looking downward is a sign of respect in Asian cultures. When in negotiations with individuals from some Asian cultures, the preference in seating arrangements is to be side by side, whereas sitting across from one another is more favored in the United States.

Although many cultures today are incorporating a Western approach or a combination of both cultures, the buyer who makes the effort to learn about the culture of the vendor (or any business partner) will have a negotiation advantage over those who don't.

CHAPTER 9

STEP SIX

Examine Income Statement

IN THIS CHAPTER, YOU WILL LEARN:

* How an income statement relates to a buyer's performance
* How an income statement is used as a decision-making tool
* To calculate profit or loss using given information

Most individuals (employees and students in particular) view the concept of profits as the dollars generated by a business over and above operating expenses, which directly benefit the owners or upper management. Hence, they do not concern themselves with the income statement of their organizations. Why should they concern themselves with profits when profits have no bearing on them?

PROFIT OR LOSS?

As you progress into management, your focus will broaden to incorporate your store's income statement. This document provides you with a view of the financial health of your company. It is become a pivotal decision-making tool and the mirror of the ultimate success or failure of you and your store. Buyers use these data to compare their departments' performance with other similar operations.

Gross margin, calculated prior to deducting operating expenses, will be the indicator of your skills as a department store buyer. As a manager, attainment of the bottom-line profit or loss will necessitate decisions on your part. The income statement offers the big picture and is a necessary part of a retailer's education.

Profit (or loss) often influences management decisions and *does* have a direct bearing on employees' salaries. Management makes salary decisions based on dollar profits. Will all employees get a cost-of-living increase? Will those same employees receive merit raises? Profits or losses will probably play a major role in this and many more management decisions. Another example might be the assignment of square footage to a department based on its profitability. If a department increases its sales and profits, the departmental square footage will often be increased, too.

COMPONENTS OF THE INCOME STATEMENT

Figure 9.1 is an example of an abbreviated or simplified income or operating statement. As implied, this document presents information related to how much income is generated and how dollars are spent to operate a retail organization. Four elements constitute the "profit mix": sales volume, cost of goods sold, operating expenses, and net other income.

Sales

Sales volume is determined by multiplying the unit retail price times the number of units sold.

EXAMPLE

$17 unit price × 100 units = $1,700

Gross sales are the total sales before any adjustments have been made in response to customer returns, customer allowances, and sales discounts.

Gross sales minus customer returns (credits or cash), customer allowances (reductions in the original price due to damaged merchandise), and sales discounts (employee discounts, preferred customers, etc.) equal net sales.

	Gross sales	$50,000
–	Customer returns, allowances, & discounts	$ 5,000
=	Net sales	$45,000

Cost of Goods Sold

Cost of goods sold is determined by the invoice price of the merchandise sold plus transportation plus alteration or assembly costs. Note that those costs involved in preparing merchandise to be sold must be added to the invoice price. Alterations such as hemming of mens' trousers or assembly of a microwave cart would be considered a cost of merchandise or goods sold.

($ in 1,000s)

Gross Sales	$225,000		
– Returns, Allowances, & Discounts	5,000		
NET SALES		$220,000	100%
Cost of Goods Sold			
Opening Inventory	70,000		
Purchases	150,000		
+ Inward Freight	400		
Total Goods Handled	220,400		
– Closing Inventory	106,000		
NET COST OF GOODS SOLD		$114,400	52%
GROSS MARGIN		$105,600	48%
OPERATING EXPENSES		$96,800	44%
Direct			
Indirect			
NET PROFIT BEFORE TAXES		$8,800	4%

FIGURE 9.1   Perry's income statement for last year

Invoice amount of merchandise sold	$3,000
+ Alterations	$ 250
+ Freight	$ 50
− 8% cash discount	$ 240
= Cost of goods sold	$3,060

Gross Margin

The difference between the net sales and the cost of goods sold is *gross margin.* This is often the bottom line for departmental buyers who have little or no control over store operating expenses. Buyers are often given a gross margin percentage to achieve and are evaluated by comparing the actual versus planned gross margin percentage.

Net sales	$50,000	100%
− Cost of goods sold	$25,000	50%
= Gross margin	$25,000	50%

Operating Expenses

Operating expenses are the costs attributed to the operations of the organization. Salary, rent, and utilities are operating expenses. There are two types of operating expenses: indirect (or fixed) and direct (or variable). Our perspective is that of a retail buyer who operates the department as an individual profit center.

Fixed expenses are those that do not vary from month to month. For the departmental buyer, these include upper-management salaries, insurance, utilities, etc. *Variable expenses* are expenses the buyer can manipulate: departmental salaries, advertising, and rent per square foot of allotted floor space.

Net sales		$50,000	100%
− Cost of goods sold		$25,000	50%
= Gross margin		$25,000	50%
− Operating expenses		$20,000	
Direct	$12,000		
Indirect	$8,000		
= Operating profit		$5,000	

Net Other Income

Net other income are those monies generated from sources other than the sale of merchandise. Examples might be interest charges from a store's credit card operations, interest earned on investments, or stock dividends. These components combine to create an operating or income statement as shown here:

Gross sales	$105,000	
– Customer returns & allowances	$ 5,000	
= Net sales	$100,000	100%
– Cost of goods sold	$ 50,000	50%
= Gross margin	$ 50,000	50%
– Operating expenses	$ 45,000	45%
= Operating profit	$ 5,000	5%
+ Other income	$ 1,000	1%
= Net profit	$ 6,000	6%

Note that both dollars and percentages are used to express the components. Percentages provide a better point of comparison than do dollars.

For example, Company A generates $10,000 in profit, whereas Company B generates $8,000 in profits. Which one is operating more efficiently? We must look beyond dollars (see the example below) to understand the complete profit picture.

Company B earned 8 percent profit, while Company A earned 5 percent; therefore, we could surmise that Company B operates more efficiently, or at least effectively.

	COMPANY A		COMPANY B	
Net sales	$200,000	100%	$100,000	100%
– Cost of goods sold	$ 100,000	50%	$ 50,000	50%
= Gross margin	$ 100,000	50%	$ 50,000	50%
– Expenses	$ 90,000	45%	$ 42,000	42%
= Profit	$ 10,000	5%	$ 8,000	8%

CHAPTER 10

The Buyer's Role in Product Development

IN THIS CHAPTER, YOU WILL LEARN:

* The changes in the buyer's responsibilities with regard to product development
* The steps of the product development process as they impact the buyer
* How private-label merchandise improves gross margin
* The skills and knowledge a buyer must have or develop to meet the demands of the product development process

As the gross margin and the "bottom line" have become the driving force of businesses, buyers must look for new ways of creating a competitive edge in the marketplace. Developing merchandise specifically for their *target customer* under a *private label* (*store brand*) or with exclusive distribution rights has become the buyers' way of increasing their profit margins while giving their customers exactly what they want.

BACKGROUND

With the vertical integration and horizontal growth of retailers, globalization, economies of scale in both retailing and apparel manufacturing, and market specialization, the role of the retail buyer has changed dramatically in the last 20 years. These market changes have precipitated major changes in the responsibilities of today's buyer.

Today, buyers must have comprehensive knowledge of their target customer including demographics, psychographics, style, color, and fabric preferences, as well as price points that the market will bear. Buyers must stay current with trends in styling, fabric, and fiber development, quality control and production issues, market information, domestic and international current events, and socioeconomic trends that may affect the purchase of their merchandise or the development of a new category. Armed with extensive market research and knowledge of both consumer preferences and the market, the buyer is ready to take part in the many interrelated steps of the product development process.

PLANNING

Planning is the first and most critical step of the product development process. Simply stated, buyers must determine the right merchandise for their consumer. Based on research, market knowledge, instinct, and experience, the buyer and the design team (depending on the size of the organization) brainstorm the attributes and styling of the upcoming product line. This meeting might include the discussion of aspects such as style and color trends, silhouettes, fabrication, customer preferences, competing brands, pricing, projected unit sales volume, and innovative ideas to obtain a competitive advantage over branded merchandise. Using the information from this meeting, design and concept boards are developed and presented for several product lines or collections for an upcoming season. Depending on the classification of merchandise and the type and size of the organization, as few as two product lines could be developed or as many as twelve to ensure a constant flow of new merchandise on a monthly basis. However, most organizations develop four to five seasonal product lines in a given year for specific departments or classifications.

Salability

At the presentation of the design or concept boards, buyers are primarily concerned with the salability of the merchandise. Their focus is getting the right merchandise to the customer at the right price and at the right time. The previous year's best-selling items are reviewed, and lost sales from underplanning are discussed. The team of designers and merchandisers edit the proposed collections and designs, and discuss the fabrication of each of the merchandise groups. They determine the number of collections needed and which collection will be delivered to the sales floor first.

Fabric

Fabric selection is based on characteristics that the consumer desires as well as the cost and availability of the fabric or an alternative selection. This is where a buyer's knowledge of textiles becomes critical. Buyers must understand performance characteristics such as wearability, care requirements, construction constraints, drape, colorfastness, and dye issues. They must also be aware of sourcing issues such as country quotas, if the fabric is to be imported, and time constraints related to the shipping costs to the factory for production. Price and terms and the availability of fabric are key to meeting production deadlines and profit goals.

Specification and Costing Sheets

From this point, samples or prototypes are made for a final review of that season's product assortment. *Specification (spec) sheets* or technical drawings are developed to outline fabrication, costing, sourcing, and specific production notes or instructions. The spec sheets are a critical part of the buyer's job because they ensure that the merchandise is made correctly. They are the blueprints for the factory to build the merchandise to the buyer's exact specifications. These sheets include the exact measurements for each size and how those measurements are made (i.e., ½ inch from the neckline), the number of sizes to be made (sizes 3–13), the assigned style number, the tolerance of deviation from the specifications (no more than ¼ inch), the cutting instructions, the detail instructions for topstitching or pocket placement, the labeling, and the detailed sketch of the item (see Figure 10.1). Details are the key to production success, and the buyer is the detail person in the product development process.

The specification sheets are also the key to quality control and assurance. The buyer is focused on many quality issues including pattern and fit of the garment, construction, finishing, and, of course, fabrication. A first sample is tried on a fitting model to check for fit and to make any necessary adjustments to the pattern before it goes into production. A buyer must also check the finishing of seams, the type and number of stitches per inch, as well as the lining, buttonholes, zippers, etc. Placement of pockets and/or trim and repeat patterns within the fabric all must be checked for accuracy. This sample must be reproducable in a factory with minimal room for error. The sample garment and production garment should be identical. Sometimes buyers will travel to factories to check production and ensure quality of the finished goods.

Costing sheets are also developed, often by the buyer, detailing all expenses involved in the manufacture of the goods. These worksheets are also used to determine the price at which the goods will retail. Information on the cost sheets includes the type of fabric, the manufacturer of that fabric, the amount of fabric, and the cost per yard of fabric per unit. Trim and *findings*, notions such as zippers, labels, buttons, and/or belts, are specified and priced. Labor costs are calculated, including marking, grading, cutting, finishing, and construction costs. If the merchandise is imported, then import duties and additional shipping costs must be calculated. From this final figure a retail

PERRY'S

MEN'S WEAR							
SIZE	34	36	38	40	42	44	46
CHEST	36	38	40	42	44	46	48
BUST							
BUST FRONT ARC							
WAIST	30	32	34	36	38	40	42
HIPS @ 4"	35	37	39	41	43	45	47
HIPS @ 8"	37	39	41	43	45	47	49
LENGTH WAIST BACK	16 3/4	17	17 1/4	17 1/2	17 3/4	18	18 1/4
LENGTH WAIST FRONT	14 1/4	14 1/2	14 3/4	15	15 1/4	15 1/2	15 3/4
ACROSS SHOULDER	16 1/2	17	17 1/2	18	18 1/2	19	19 1/2
ACROSS BACK @ 4"	15 1/2	16	16 1/2	17	17 1/2	18	18 1/2
ACROSS CHEST @ 1 1/2"	15	15 1/2	16	16 1/2	17	17 1/2	18
DIAPHRAGM UNDER BUST							
DIAPHRAGM MIDWAY							
SHOULDER							
BUST AROUND NECK							
NECK	14 3/4	15 1/4	15 3/4	16 1/4	16 3/4	17 1/4	17 3/4
CROTCH W.W.	27	28	29	30	31	32	33
MAX THIGH	22	23	24	25	26	27	28
MIDDLE THIGH							
KNEE	15	15 1/2	16	16 1/2	17	17 1/2	18
CALF	14	14 1/2	15	15 1/2	16	16 1/2	17
ANKLE							
ANKLE LENGTH							
WAIST TO KNEE							
WAIST TO FLOOR							
CROTCH HEIGHT—ANKLE	29 5/8	29 3/4	29 7/8	30	30 1/8	30 1/4	30 3/8
KNEE HEIGHT							
ACROSS BUST							
B.M.S.							

FIGURE 10.1 Perry's specification sheet for men's wear

price can be calculated based on a targeted gross margin percentage or markup. If the proposed retail price of the merchandise is too high for the target customer, the buyer or merchandiser must make adjustments to make the item more salable. The buyer may suggest different buttons or a less expensive fabric, even a different factory or country of origin, while still maintaining the integrity of the original design concept. See Figure 10.2 for a domestic costing sheet, and Figure 10.3 for an import product sheet.

SOURCING

Another critical element of the buyer's job in some companies is the sourcing of all the elements that make up a finished product. The buyer may be responsible for procuring all the fabric, trims, and buttons and must coordinate the delivery of these items to the factory where the garment or item is to be produced. Considering the global nature of the apparel and accessory business and the gift industry, these different components probably come from all over the world, and the coordination of their timely arrival is critical to production deadlines. Due to the competitive nature of the fashion industry and its labor-intensive product, sourcing has become a global endeavor. Labor costs are significantly lower in certain parts of the world, and government initiatives encourage the use of foreign factories, fabrics, and findings. Buyers must be knowledgeable of *quotas* such as the *General Agreement on Tariffs and Trade (GATT)* and now the *World Trade Organization (WTO)* guidelines. They must also understand how and what duties are charged on imported products, and the numerous agreements impacting trade such as the *North American Free Trade Agreement (NAFTA)* and the *Caribbean Basin Initiative (CBI)*. Buyers must stay abreast of political and economic issues that might affect production at a factory in another part of the world, and they must be sensitive to human right issues related to work, such as child labor and health, and safety issues. Many retailers such as Kmart and Wal-Mart have received negative publicity because the factories used to produce their merchandise violated the human rights of local workers in developing nations. This is another reason that buyers often visit factories in other parts of the world.

Testing

Another issue of concern for the buyer is the testing of fabrication and construction of the merchandise to be manufactured. The buyer must have the fabric tested to make sure it meets the specifications detailed on the spec sheets. There are numerous test services or facilities that will test fabric flammability, fabric performance, and actual

PERRY'S

Piece Goods Cost/Yard		$	9.00	
Freight to Sponger & Contractor	+	$	0.50	
Sponging Cost/Yard	+	$	0.35	
Cost per Yard	=	$	9.85	
Yield	×		3.5	
TOTAL PIECE GOODS COST				$ 34.48
CMT	+	$	45.00	
Upcharges	+	$	2.00	
(DB, plaids, elbow patches, etc.)				
TOTAL PRODUCTION COSTS				$ 47.00
Hanger	+	$	0.60	
Labels	+	$	0	
Poly Bag	+	$	0	
Hanger Box	+	$	0	
Freight	+	$	0.50	
Trademark Charge	+	$	1.00	
Additional Financing	+	$	1.00	
TOTAL OTHER COSTS				$ 3.10
TOTAL COST DELIVERED				$ 84.58
UNIT RETAIL				$ 219.95	$ 199.95
INITIAL MARK-ON				61.50%	57.70%

FIGURE 10.2   Perry's costing sheet

Date: 1/15/09	**Season:** Fall 2009
Dept: Gifts	
Buyer: K. Smith	
Phone: 703-555-1212	
E-mail: ksmith@perrys.com	

Manufacturer Name & Address: Domore	**Contact:** Christina
	Phone:
	Fax:
	E-mail:

Agent Name:	**Commission:**
Item #: 43278	**Description:** Decorative black metal plate rack with 4 nautical asst. 8" plates, vertical, 39.75" L × 11.5" W
Port: Shenzhen	
Lead Time: 90 days	
Minimum: 1,200 units	**Materials/Fiber Content % Weight:** Metal plate rack, powder coated; ceramic plates
Cube: 3.0	
Inner: 1	
Master: 4	**Tariff Number:** 7326.2000.70
40' Container Qty: 2,664	**Carton Meas. L: W: H:**
20' Container Qty:	**UPC#:** 055176432780
Unit of Measure: each	
FOB U.S. $ Cost: $6.75	
Freight: 1.50	$2.00 per cu.ft.
Duty: 26.0%	3.90%
Misc.: 0.34	5% of F.O.B. cost
Landed Cost: 8.85	
Retail: $24.99	**64.6% margin**

color photo here

Units Ordering: 2,664

FIGURE 10.3   Perry's import product sheet

performance of the garment. These are critical issues that ensure the salability of the merchandise and its entry into the United States.

Labeling

Labeling requirements are also of concern to buyers. U.S. law requires that all apparel merchandise sold in the United States be labeled with fabric content, country of origin, and care instructions. The placement of this label is also critical to the wearability of the garment.

Shipping

The product mix requires that the buyer get the merchandise to the consumer at the "right time." Shipping arrangements are important, especially for goods made outside the United States. The buyer must determine whether the goods should be shipped by air or boat, and the cost will impact the profitability of the goods. The documentation that must accompany imported goods is significant and includes such items as quota visa, commercial invoice, bill of lading, packing slip, and surety bond. If any of the documentation is incorrect or missing, the shipment could be held up for weeks, which could negatively affect the salability of the goods due to the seasonal nature of fashion. Import agents often manage much of this process because they are closer to the merchandise or are in frequent contact with the factory. These agents are usually fluent in the native language of the region where the factory is located and are also specialists in exporting goods from the country of origin to the United States.

Technology

As product development buyers' responsibilities continue to evolve, so does the technology that assists them in managing the process. *Computer-aided design (CAD) systems* allow merchandise to be created on a 2- and 3-D basis, and create patterns that will account for fabric properties and anomalies. Textile prints can be created and placed on specific garments to maximize fabric use and efficiency. A factory in Japan can show a prototype garment with a choice of fabric, findings, and style variations via a networked system, live telecast, or downloadable images from the Internet. Changes can be made immediately, and communication difficulties (e.g., language differences) can be clarified.

Product management systems help the buyer create product development calendars, style descriptions, cost sheets, specification sheets, quality control data, vendor quote analyses, and standard measurement tables, as well as manage sourcing and transportation information. The buyer must master new technologies to remain competitive in an industry that is demanding shorter and shorter *lead times* and delivery times of new merchandise.

SUMMARY

Product development has added an exciting but demanding dimension to the buyer's job. Not only does it allow the buyer to be more creative, but it requires in-depth knowledge of production cycles, product construction, and fabrication. Buyers must recognize great design, but also understand the limitations placed by financial constraints, gross margin projections, international quotas, global economic conditions, and current events. A buyer must be sensitive to cross-cultural nuances that can make or break a deal while negotiating a smart bargain that creates a win-win situation for both organizations. Today's buyer must be detail oriented, technologically savvy, culturally sensitive, and creatively inclined.

CHAPTER 11

Career Opportunities in Retail Buying

IN THIS CHAPTER, YOU WILL LEARN:

* The different types of buying careers and career paths
* The entry-, mid-, and upper-level buying positions
* The roles, skills, and responsibilities of buying positions

This chapter details the job titles and corresponding job requirements available in retail buying. Beginning with entry-level, trainee positions and concluding at the level of general merchandise manager, it is a helpful section for the student. Other aspects are touched upon as well—the broadening areas of buying, the availability of trainee programs, and the opportunities in buying groups.

OVERVIEW

Although the role of the retail buyer generally remains consistent from small to large stores, the number of positions that assist buying activities varies. The larger the store operation, the more levels of opportunity are available. In larger corporations, buyers may be accountable for as much as $50 million or more in sales volume. Retail buying jobs have broadened to include more positions in merchandise analysis and planning to assist the buyer in controlling high volume. In many stores, the career path to the level of buyer and above weaves back and forth between the store operation and the buying division. Focusing on the buying division, many operations further divide responsibility between buying and merchandising/planning.

Numerous department and chain stores recruit college graduates to join their executive training programs. College graduates are hired on an executive level and receive on-the-job training for entry-level executive positions. Merchandise assistant, coordinator, analyst, and allocator are some of the typical entry-level jobs for college graduates in the buying division.

Merchandise Assistant, Merchandise Coordinator

All buyers require administrative support. Clerical duties characteristic of this job include distributing store orders, tracking orders to be sure they are delivered on time, instituting markdowns on seasonal and slow-moving items, obtaining samples for advertising, and handling return-to-vendor merchandise. At HSN, the television shopping network, a merchandise assistant is also responsible for transporting samples to QA for quality assurance testing and managing the sample room with product for upcoming shows.

Qualifications

Qualifications required for the position are strong organizational and communication skills, high motivation, and the ability to handle multiple tasks. Computer experience in Excel and Word is essential. At Target Corporation, new merchandise coordinators enroll in a six-week training course for their positions. Courses are available to strengthen computer skills and to learn management techniques.

Business Analyst, Merchandise Analyst, or Merchandise Allocator

The analyst or allocator is responsible for managing inventory and allocating merchandise to the stores. An important duty is to review and reorder basic stock. Another task is to detect best-sellers and identify slow-moving items. Sales and stock are analyzed to forecast sales projections and plan assortments. The analyst or allocator communicates with vendors, checks on orders, and exchanges information on stock and sales. Merchandise allocators for S&K Menswear manage the Quick Response program, identifying and reordering best sellers as sales are rung at the register. At Marshall Field's and Target Corporation, a business analyst advances to senior business analyst on the career path.

Qualifications

The entry-level position of business analyst, merchandise analyst, or merchandise allocator requires a college degree or previous retail or business experience. Qualifications of the job include strong analytical, decision-making, planning, and problem-solving skills. The candidate should possess good communication and organizational skills and exhibit strong initiative. The next step for a merchandise analyst at Lord and Taylor is assistant buyer.

Planner

Within the merchandising/planning track, the role of the planner is to plan and regulate inventory. By analyzing past sales and inventory history, the planner forecasts trends to maximize sales and profit.

In Federated Department Stores, such as Macy's and Bloomingdale's, the planner works with the buying team and individual store locations to develop assortment plans for a core vendor, specific area, or department. The planner identifies key items, plans purchases, allocates merchandise to appropriate locations, and monitors stock levels for replenishment. Reorders for stock replenishment are presented to the buyer. A planner at HSN, the television shopping network plans the strategy and forecasts inventory for shows. Together with the buying and programming team, the planner helps to identify new business and key items. Following the show, a recap is presented to the buyer. The planner handles reorders and disposition of remaining goods after the show.

Qualifications

Qualifications for this position include excellent written and oral communication skills, detail orientation, strong analytical abilities, and computer competency in Word and Excel.

Both Macy's and Bloomingdale's offer planning executive trainee programs. A trainee can advance from assistant planner to associate planner to planner.

Manager of Planning and Distribution

A manager of planning and distribution (MPD) works with the divisional merchandise manager (DMM) and buying team, and oversees a team of planners. The manager provides guidance for the merchandise division to effectively plan, distribute, and monitor inventory levels by store location. The goal is to maximize sales, maintain proper turnover, and increase profit. The manager works with the team to formulate strategies to accomplish set objectives.

Qualifications

Qualifications for this position are four to seven years' experience as a planner or buyer and several years' experience as a supervisor. The manager must have excellent analytical and communication skills.

Director of Distribution and Planning

The director of distribution and planning (DDP) supervises the MPD and planning team. This position is accountable for achieving sales and profit goals for a specific business. The director assists in developing strategies and seeking opportunities to meet financial objectives and location plans. The director works closely with the buying team to direct assortment planning.

Qualifications

The requirements for a DDP position are four to seven years of retail planning or buying and several years of supervising a team. As in other planning jobs, a director must have strong analytical skills, good written and oral communication skills, and an ability to form partnerships and communicate with all levels of the organization.

Assistant Buyer

The assistant buyer manages the buying office and supports the buyer in all aspects of business. Depending on the buyer's volume and breadth of responsibility, the assistant may undertake buying for a classification. Assistants are accountable for monitoring delivery of purchase orders and communicating with both the distribution center and the vendors. The buyer relies on the assistant to analyze the business and prepare recaps and reports. Stock levels are examined for appropriate distribution. The assistant advises the buyer and stores of best sellers and key items. Other tasks are to identify slow sellers and seasonal merchandise and plan markdowns within the budget. Assistants take part in advertising preparation by completing ad requests, obtaining samples from vendors, submitting items for ads at advertising meetings, proofing ads, and recapping results. Depending on the proximity of the market, the buyer may request the assistant to attend markets.

Qualifications

An assistant buyer must be able to work in a fast-paced environment, be detail oriented and organized, possess superb analytical skills, and have strong oral and written communication skills. Computer experience is required with proficiency in Word and Excel.

Associate Buyer, Senior Assistant Buyer

The next step to buyer is the position of associate buyer or senior assistant buyer, depending on what title the store may use. The associate or senior assistant is accountable for managing and buying for an assigned area. This includes developing pricing and promotional strategy for the area, formulating the dollar merchandise plan, shopping the market to identify trends and merchandise opportunities, and negotiating with vendors. The associate or senior assistant works with planners on assortments and distribution. Recommendations for merchandise presentation are presented to the visual merchandising team.

Qualifications

For this position, the candidate should be detail-oriented, have strong analytical skills, be effective in oral and written communication skills, have knowledge of basic retail math and computer skills, and be able to work well with others. At least 18 months or more of experience as an assistant buyer are required.

Buyer

The buyer is responsible for planning, managing, and achieving financial objectives for one or more departments of the store. The company holds the buyer accountable for meeting sales, markdowns, gross margin, and turnover goals. The buyer develops the merchandising and marketing strategy for the area of business, supervises the procurement of merchandise, builds relationships with vendors, monitors performance of merchandise and vendors, and provides direction for visual presentation. Buyers work closely with the planning team to create proper assortment plans and to advise on distribution. Training of assistant and associate buyers is a task for the buyer.

Qualifications

To become a buyer, two or more years of experience is required, depending on the size of the business area and the store organization. Qualifications include abilities in strategic planning and forecasting, strong analytical skills, good written and oral communication skills, and the ability to effectively communicate with all levels of management. Buyers need to be detail-oriented, have a sense of urgency, and be adept in handling multiple tasks.

Divisional Merchandise Manager

Buyers report to a divisional merchandise manager (DMM). The DMM oversees the implementation of the merchandise strategy and financial goals for specific merchandise divisions such as men's wear or home furnishings. It is the responsibility of this position to direct the buyers in merchandise selection and purchasing for all areas within the division. The DMM provides the vision and ensures that the strategy and goals meet company plans. The planning team looks to the DMM for direction in assortment planning and location distribution. The DMM works with buyers to build their relationships with vendors. It is the duty of the DMM to provide support and to promote the growth of the buyer. The person in this position must also be aware of competitors and their strengths and weaknesses.

Qualifications
Experience of four or more years in buying or merchandising and a minimum of several years of supervising a team are required for the position of DMM. The DMM must exhibit strong leadership and negotiation skills. The person should be organized, able to compete in a fast-paced environment, demonstrate strong analytical skills and excellent oral and written communication skills, and have the ability to build teams and develop partnerships.

General Merchandise Manager
The general merchandise managers (GMMs) oversee more than one division, with the DMM reporting to them. Typically, a store has a GMM for soft goods and a GMM for hard lines. Duties and qualifications are the same as those of the DMM.

Buying Groups and Services
Some larger department stores and chains operate their own buying and sourcing organizations. Macy's Merchandising Group employs a design and production team to design and source private label brands for the Macy's, Inc., stores. The group also works together with buyers to source product from national brands. Target Sourcing Services/AMC sources product from overseas for Target buyers. Design and merchandising services include product development to production of merchandise.

Many stores rely on the expertise of external buying groups and services to provide guidance in retail buying and merchandising. The Doneger Group and Kurt Salmon Associates are two well-known consulting companies that provide trend information and merchandising planning for their customers. Li and Fung Limited is a sourcing operation based in Hong Kong that sources apparel and home furnishings product from overseas for customers. For additional information on buying groups and services, go to www.apparelsearch.com/buying_groups.htm.

To research job opportunities through the Internet, use a search engine such as Google. Type the name of the store or buying organization of interest in the search box. Most Web sites have a tab for careers within that company. Another good source of job opportunities is the classified section of trade magazines. For a general search of career openings, you may find the following Web sites helpful:

About.com

Careerbuilder.com

Monster.com

24seventalent.com

APPENDIX A

Web Site Resources

Following is a selection of organizations and their corresponding Internet addresses relating to retail buying. Readers may wish to use a search engine such as Google, or a directory like Yahoo! to find additional relevant Web sites. Be aware that new sites are launched constantly while others disappear just as quickly.

BUYING GROUPS AND MAJOR RETAIL STORES

Bed Bath & Beyond:
www.bedbathandbeyond.com

Belk Stores: www.belk.com

Bloomingdale's: www.bloomingdales.com

Bon-Ton: www.bonton.com

Boscov's: www.boscov.com

Dillard's: www.dillards.com

The Doneger Group: www.doneger.com

Elder-Beerman:
www.elder-beerman.com

FredMeyer: www.fredmeyer.com

Gap: www.gap.com

Gottschalks: www.gottschalks.com

HSN: www.hsn.com

JCPenney: www.jcpenney.com

Kohl's: www.kohls.com

Limited Brands: www.limited.com

Linens 'n Things: www.lnt.com

Macy's: www.macysinc.com

Nordstrom: www.nordstrom.com

Peebles: www.peebles.com

QVC: www.iqvc.com

S&K Menswear: www.skmenswear.com

Saks: www.saksincorporated.com

Sears: www.sears.com

Stage Stores: www.stagestores.com

Target: www.target.com

Target Sourcing Services: www.theamc.com

Wal-Mart: www.walmart.com

INDUSTRY RESOURCES

American Wool Council:
www.americanwool.org
American Apparel and
Footwear Association:
www.apparelandfootwear.org
Apparel Search: www.apparelsearch.com
Cotton Incorporated: www.cottoninc.com
National Retail Federation: www.nrf.com
Pantone: www.pantone.com

Market Centers and Trade Show Information

AmericasMart: www.americasmart.com
Buylink: www.buylink.com
CaliforniaMart: www.californiamart.com
Dallas Market Center:
www.dallasmarketcenter.com
The Fashion Center:
www.fashioncenter.com
George Little Management:
www.glmshows.com
MAGIC (Men's Apparel
Guild in California):
www.magiconline.comMerchandise
Mart Properties:
www.merchandisemart.com

Trade Publications and Trend Information

Accessory Merchandising:
www.accessorymerchandising.com
Apparel News: www.apparelnews.net
The Doneger Group: www.doneger.com
Fairchild Publications:
www.fairchildpub.com
Fashion Snoops: www.fashionsnoops.com
Furniture Style: www.furniturestyle.com
Giftbeat: www.giftbeat.com
Gifts & Decorative Accessories:
www.giftsanddec.com
Giftware News: www.giftwarenews.com

Home Accents Today:
www.homeaccentstoday.com
Home Furnishings News (*HFN*):
www.hfnmag.com
Infomat Fashion Calendar: www.infomat.com
Just Style: www.just-style.com
Label Networks: www.labelnetworks.com
National Retail Federation: www.nrf.com
Stores: www.stores.org
The Trend Curve: www.trendcurve.com
Trend Stop: www.trendstop.com
Trend Zine: www.fashioninformation.com
WeAr Global Magazine:
www.wear-magazine.com
Worth Global Source Network:
www.wgsn.com
Women's Wear Daily: www.wwd.com
WWDMen's:
www.wwd.com/menswear-news

Consumer Marketing

Advertising Age: www.adage.com
CRMTalk (Customer Relationship
Management): www.crmguru.com/
crmtalk/2002a/crmt149.htm
Claritas Inc.: www.claritas.com
KnowThis.com, Marketing Virtual Library:
www.knowthis.com
New Media Broadcasters: www.nmbi.com

Consumer Demographics/ Psychographics

Celebrate Virginia:
www.celebratevirginia.com
Podunk: www.podunk.com
About.Com: Retail Industry:
www.retailindustry.about.com
Silver Company: silvercompany.com
SRI Consulting Business Intelligence:
www.sric-bi.com/VALS/
Virginia Workforce Connection:
www.vaworkconnect.com

Retailing Formulas

Planned Sales Increase/Decrease

Dollar increase = LY sales × Planned % increase

Dollar increase	TY planned sales
+ LY sales	– LY actual sales
= Planned sales	= Sales increase

Planned Sales Increase Percentage

$$\text{Percentage increase} = \frac{\text{Dollar increase}}{\text{LY actual sales}}$$

Stock-to-Sales Ratio

$$\text{Stock-to-sales ratio} = \frac{\text{Retail stock at a given time}}{\text{Sales for the period}}$$

BOM Stock

BOM stock = Planned sales × Stock/sales ratio

Turnover

$$\text{Turnover} = \frac{\text{Net sales for period}}{\text{Average inventory or stock for same period}}$$

Average Stock

$$\text{Average stock} = \frac{\text{Sum of BOM stock} + \text{Ending stock (EOM)}}{\text{Number of inventories (BOM stock)}}$$

Planned Purchases

    Planned sales
+ Planned EOM stock
+ Planned markdowns
– Planned BOM stock
= Planned purchases at retail

Planned Purchases at Cost

Planned purchases at cost = Planned purchases at retail × (100% – Markup %)

Open-to-buy

    Planned purchases
– Outstanding purchase orders not yet delivered
= Open-to-buy

Open-to-buy at Cost

Open-to-buy at cost = Open-to-buy at retail × (100% – Markup %)

Sales Volume

Sales volume = Unit retail price × Number of units sold

Net Sales

    Gross sales
– Customer returns, allowances, and discounts
= Net sales

Cost of Goods Sold

Invoice amount of merchandise sold
+ Alterations
+ Freight
− 8% cash discount
_____
= Cost of goods sold

Gross Margin

Net sales
− Cost of goods sold
_____
= Gross margin

Total Operating Expenses

Direct expenses
+ Indirect expenses
_____
= Total operating expenses

Sales Recap

Pre = ad on = hand units/dollars
− Post = ad on = hand units/dollars
_____
= Total units/dollars sold

$$\frac{\text{Total units/dollars sold}}{\text{Pre = ad on = hand units/dollars}} = \text{Percentage of sell through}$$

Glossary

anticipation An additional discount granted for payment of an invoice prior to the due date.

assistant buyer The assistant buyer manages the buying office and supports the buyer in all aspects of business. Depending on the volume of the buyer and breadth of responsibility, the assistant may undertake buying for a classification.

associate buyer The associate buyer or senior assistant is accountable for managing and buying for an assigned area in the buying office.

assortment plan The breakdown of merchandise by classification.

average stock (average inventory) The sum of the retail inventories divided by the number of inventories in the period examined (month, season, or year).

balanced stock Stock sufficient to meet planned sales without overstocking the department.

bulk estimate An estimate of total units per style that a store buyer might purchase. The estimate of the style may not be detailed by color, size, or individual branch store for shipping.

business analyst The analyst or allocator is a position in the buying office that is responsible for managing inventory and allocating merchandise to the stores.

buyer The buyer is responsible for planning, managing, and achieving financial objectives for one or more departments of the retail store.

Caribbean Basin Initiative (CBI) Government regulation that will treat the nations in the Caribbean Basin similar to Mexico as under the *NAFTA* agreement.

cash discount A percentage of deduction taken for paying an invoice within the specified time allowed.

classification A type of merchandise such as dresses or skirts.

classification report A sales report provided to buyers by classification such as sales of skirts for a specified period of time.

closeouts Merchandise that is marked down for clearance.

computer-aided design (CAD) system A computer system that allows designers to create both two- and three-dimensional designs on the computer.

cost of goods sold Determined by the invoice price of merchandise sold plus transportation plus alternation or assembly costs.

costing sheets Forms used to estimate all costs associated with the construction and production of a garment or item.

dating Amount of time allowed for payment of an invoice.

director of distribution and planning (DDP) This buying position is responsible for supervising the MPD and the planning team and for achieving sales and profit goals of a specific business.

divisional merchandise manager (DMM) Managerial person responsible for a group of buyers and their specific merchandise categories.

drop paper An order placed with a vendor or wholesaler usually at a sales appointment while the buyer is in the market.

electronic data interchange (EDI) Computerized communication network between retailer, manufacturer, and other supply chain members.

EOM dating Dating computed from the end of the month.

extra dating Allowance of a longer period of time to pay an invoice and still receive a discount.

findings Notions such as zippers, labels, buttons, and/or belts.

fixed expenses Costs that do not vary from month to month.

FOB (free on board) factory Delivery term whereby the store takes ownership of merchandise once the goods leave the manufacturer's factory; the store is also responsible for all freight charges and insurance.

FOB point Location where the merchandise changes ownership from manufacturer to store.

FOB store Delivery term whereby the manufacturer retains ownership of and responsibility for merchandise until it reaches the store; the manufacturer thus pays all freight charges and insurance.

General Agreement on Tariffs and Trade (GATT) An agreement (1947) among many countries to reduce trade barriers and unify trading practices. In 1995, it was replaced by the *World Trade Organization (WTO)*.

general merchandise manager (GMM) Management person responsible for specific merchandise divisions. Oversees divisional merchandise managers.

gross margin Dollar amount of profit after subtracting costs of merchandise sold from total net sales; difference between net sales and cost of goods sold.

gross sales Total sales before any adjustments for customer returns, customer allowances, and/or sales discounts.

incentive purchasing See *seasonal discount*.

institutional ad Advertisement in which the store logo is used along with a particular message; it sells the image and good reputation of the store rather than specific merchandise.

lead time The period of time needed to manufacture merchandise from receipt of the order to time of delivery.

manager of planning and distribution (MPD) The MPD works with the divisional merchandise manager and buying team, and oversees a team of planners. The MPD provides guidance for the merchandise division to effectively plan, distribute, and monitor inventory levels by store location.

markdown A reduction in the retail price.

market The location where vendors show and sell their merchandise to retail store buyers.

Men's Apparel Guild in California (MAGIC) A men's wear trade association that sponsors market twice a year; currently held in Las Vegas, Nevada.

merchandise allocator See *business analyst*.

merchandise analyst See *business analyst*.

merchandise assistant An assistant in the buying office who performs administrative duties. Clerical duties characteristic of this job include executing store distribution of orders, tracking orders to be sure they are delivered on time, instituting markdowns on seasonal and slow-moving items, obtaining samples for advertising, and handling return to vendor merchandise.

merchandise coordinator See *merchandise assistant*.

monochronic culture People with a preference to work on only one task at a time. Monochronic people are punctual and prefer working with a sequential plan.

National Association of Men's Sportswear Buyers (NAMSB) A men's wear trade association that sponsors market in New York several times a year and produces a newsletter.

negotiation Discussion between two or more people who work together to resolve a problem or come to terms on a deal, each having to give and take to reach a final agreement.

net other income Monies generated from sources other than the sale of merchandise.

North American Free Trade Agreement (NAFTA) An agreement that eliminated quotas and tariffs for goods shipped between Canada, Mexico, and the United States.

open-to-buy (OTB) The amount of money available to purchase merchandise that is not accounted for by previous purchase orders. Knowledge of OTB allows the buyer to regulate or adjust inventory levels according to actual sales.

operating expenses Costs attributed to the organization's operations.

planner Within the merchandising/planning track, the role of the planner is to plan and regulate inventory. By analyzing past sales and inventory history, the planner forecasts trends to maximize sales and profit.

polychronic culture People with a preference to work on multiple tasks and capable of communicating with multiple persons at the same time. Polychronic people are flexible.

price line A predetermined retail price for an assortment or classification of merchandise targeted at a specific customer base.

private label or *store brand* Merchandise that is developed exclusively for a retail store to its specifications.

quantity discount Discount extended to a buyer for ordering a large amount of merchandise.

Quick Response program A retail program that identifies and generates reorders for best sellers as sales are rung at the register.

quota A limit placed on the number of items that can be imported into the United States, by category, for each country.

receipt of goods (ROG) dating Dating as of receipt of goods; the date the merchandise is delivered to the store is used to determine the payment period.

regular dating Type of dating in which the cash discount and net periods are figured from the date of the invoice.

resident buying office An organization that provides buyers and stores with market and fashion trend advice, as well as many other services.

resource A manufacturer or vendor of merchandise.

return to vendor (RTV) Merchandise returned to the vendor due to damaged goods, incorrect shipments, or overstocks. Another term used is return to manufacturer (RTM).

rounders A type of display fixture that is round, and is used to show apparel. It is usually found in the back of a department.

sales representative Person employed by a manufacturer or wholesaler to show a line of merchandise to store buyers and to take orders on merchandise selected.

seasonal discount (incentive purchasing) Discount offered on merchandise bought prior to the normal buying season.

senior assistant buyer See *associate buyer*.

six-month dollar merchandise plan A plan that budgets dollars spent on merchandise in relation to projected sales.

sourcing Determining how and where a garment or item will be produced.

specification (spec) sheets Forms used to detail all specifications needed to produce a garment or item.

stock-to-sales ratio Inventory-planning method whereby the buyer establishes a relationship or ratio of stock (BOM) to sales on a monthly basis.

style out Method that checks for duplication or overlap used by buyers to review merchandise selected prior to writing the order.

subclassification A further division of a merchandise classification.

target customer A specific type of potential customer that either a manufacturer or a retailer is trying to reach through the development of new product.

terms of sale Final agreement for sale, as a result of negotiation between the manufacturer or wholesaler and the retail store, concerning the transportation, delivery time frame, and amount of payment for merchandise purchased.

trade discount A percentage or percentages deducted from the retail list price of merchandise.

trade publications Newspapers, magazines, or newsletters published for a specific industry, available to professionals in the field.

trade show An exhibit of merchandise for a specific period of time, during which vendors show and sell their merchandise to retail store buyers.

t-stand A type of display fixture that has two sides and is often used to show merchandise coordinates.

turnover The rate or velocity at which the average stock has been sold and the money earned reinvested into merchandise within a given period.

unit sales reports A sales report provided to buyers that denotes what has sold by style or SKU (sales keeping unit) number.

variable expenses Costs that the buyer can manipulate or change.

vendor co-op Agreement by the vendor to share the expense of advertising or a special in-store event.

vendor performance report A sales report provided to buyers that denotes sales by vendor or manufacturer. Buyers use this report to determine profitability of lines of merchandise.

waterfalls A type of display fixture that cascades merchandise and is often used to merchandise coordinating apparel.

World Trade Organization (WTO) An organization of many nations that controls trading practices, many of which involve apparel and textiles.

Bibliography

Burns, Leslie Davis, and Nancy O. Bryant. *The Business of Fashion*. 2nd ed. New York: Fairchild Books, 2002.

Cash, R. P., and H. H. Frankel. *Improving Apparel Shop Profits*. New York: National Retail Merchants Association, 1986.

Clodfelter, Richard. *Making Buying Decisions: Using the Computer as a Tool*. 2nd ed. New York: Fairchild Books, 2002.

_____. *Retail Buying: From Basics to Fashion*. 2nd ed. New York: Fairchild Books, 2002.

Davis, Kevin. "Eight Sources of Power in a Sales Negotiation." WebProNews, (2002, April). www.webpronews.com (accessed on 27 December 2007).

Diamond, Ellen. *Fashion Retailing*. New York: Delmar, 1993.

Diamond, Jay, and Ellen Diamond. *Fashion Advertising and Promotion*, New York: Fairchild Books, 1996.

Diamond, Jay, and Gerald Pintel. *Retail Buying*. 6th ed. Upper Saddle River, NJ: Prentice Hall, 2001.

Dlabay, Les, and James C. Scott. *Business in a Global Economy*. Cincinnati, Ohio: South-Western Educational Publishing, 1996.

Fiore, Ann Marie, and Patricia Anne Kimle. *Understanding Aesthetics for the Merchandising and Design Professional*. New York: Fairchild Books, 1997.

Fredricksburg Regional Alliance. "Demographics: Community Profiles." (2007). www.fra-yes.org (accessed on 20 August 2007).

Guthrie, Karen M., and Rose J. Regni (2006). *Perry's Department Store: A Product Development Simulation*. New York: Fairchild Books, 2006.

Jernigan, M. H., and C. R. Easterling. *Fashion Merchandising and Marketing*. New York: Macmillan, 1990.

Latz, Marty. "Cross-cultural negotiations present special challenges." *The Business Journal of Phoenix*. (2004, December 10). www.bizjournals.com (accessed on 27 December 2007).

LeBaron, Michelle. "Culture-Based Negotiation Styles." *Beyond Intractability* (2003, July). www.beyondintractability.org (accessed on 27 December 2007).

Lindner, Steven. *Retail Accountability: Advanced Retail Profitability Analysis*. New York: Fairchild Books, 2004.

Payne, Neil. "Cross Cultural Negotiation." *The Sideroad*. www.sideroad.com (accessed on 27 December 2007).Rosenau, Jeremy A., and David L. Wilson. *Apparel Merchandising: The Line Starts Here*. New York: Fairchild Books, 2001.

Reamy, Donna W., and Cynthia W. Steele. *Perry's Department Store: An Importing Simulation*. New York: Fairchild Books, 2006.

Solomon, Michael R., and Nancy J. Rabolt. *Consumer Behavior in Fashion*. New Jersey: Prentice Hall, 2004, p. 206.

Tepper, Bette K., and Newton E. Godnick. *Mathematics for Retail Buying*, 5th ed. revised. New York: Fairchild Books, 2002.

Virginia Employment Commission (2007, December). Virginia Work Connection: Virginia Community Profiles. www.vaworkconnect.com (accessed on 27 December 2007).

U.S. Census Bureau (2007, December). American Community Survey. www.census.gov (accessed on 27 December 2007).

Index

C

D

E

markdowns, 49; allowances, 98; and
percentage-by-month formula, 51; in
six-month dollar plans, 37, 39, 49, *53*
market assessment, 76–77
Marketing Directions, Inc., 3
market itineraries, 73–74, 80; Perry's
samples, *81–82*
market planning guide, 80, 83
market purchases: preplanning, 79–80, 83
market trips, 71–72, 80; planning for 73–75
merchandise: analysis of, 97–8
merchandise allocators, 118–19
merchandise analyst, 118
merchandise assistant/coordinator, 118
merchandise classifications, 57–58,
60; subclassifications, 60. *See also*
assortment plans
mercandise development. *See* product
development
merchandise managers: divisional merchandise managers (DMMs), 19; general merchandise managers (GMMs), 19
monochronic culture, 99
Monster.com, 123
monthly sales increase/decrease form, *45*
monthly sales: plan form, *44*; and sales by
classification, 58, 60

N

negotiation. *See* vendor negotiations
negotiation meeting, 93–94
net other income, 105–5
North American Free Trade Agreement
(NAFTA), 111

O

open-to-buy, 52, 54
operating expenses, 104

P

payment terms: negotiation of, 95
percentage-by-month formula, 51
Perry's department store: assortment plan
forms, *64–66, 68, 70*; assortment
planning factors, *63*; branch store
classifications, 17–18; classification
sales by month, *61*; consumer profile
worksheet, *30*; costing sheet, *112*;
demographic information, 2; import
product sheet, *113*; income statement,
103; markdowns worksheet, *53*;
monthly sales increase/decrease form,
45; monthly sales plan form, *44*;
organizational structure, 19–22;
purchase order, *87*; sales by classification, percentage, and dollars, *59*; sales
by store class, *18*; sales plan worksheet,
43; simulation objectives, 1–2;
six-month dollar plan, *36*; spec sheet,
110; stock/sales ratio and BOM stock
form, *50*; subclassifications, *62*; travel
itinerary samples, *81–82. See also*
Caroline County (VA); Fredericksburg,
Virginia; Spotsylvania County (VA);
Stafford County (VA)
planned markdowns. *See* markdowns
planned purchases, 39, 56, 73; preplanning, 79–80, 83

planned sales, 35. *See also* sales planning

polychronic culture, 99–100

pre-market planning, 72

price lines, 67, 70

private labels (store brands), 107

product development (buyer's role in), 107–15; background, 107–8; fabric selection, 108–9; and labeling, 114; planning, 108; salability, 108; and shipping, 114; specification and costing sheets, 109, 111; and sourcing, 111; and technology, 114–15

psychographics, 23–27. *See also* VALS survey

purchase orders, 54, 84–85; and cancellations, 98–99; Perry's example, *87*

purchases: in six-month dollar plan, 39, *54*; negotiation of, 95. *See also* buying; planned purchases

Q

quantity discounts, 86

R

receipt of goods (ROG) dating, 88

regular dating, 88

resident buying offices, 75

retail growth: researching, 42

retail trade publications, 31–32

return-to-vendor (RTV), 33, 93, 94

S

sales: by classification, 58, *59*, 60; estimating, 39; gross, 102; increase/decrease form, *45*; in six-month dollar plan, 35, 39, 42–43; volume, 102. *See also* sales planning

sales planning; in six-month dollar plan 39, 42–43; monthly sales plan form, *44*. *See also* six-month dollar plans

sales plan worksheet, *43*

sales representative, 84

sales volume (calculation of), 102

Sears: and Hispanic market, 28

seasonal discounts, 86

shipping, 114

six-month dollar plans, 35, 79; budget planning, 42; components, 35, 37; and 4-5-4 calendars, 37; monthly sales plan form, *44*; objectives, 37; and open-to-buy system, 52, 54; purchases worksheet, *55*; Perry's format, *36*. *See also* buying plans

Soldi, Thalia, 28

sourcing: and labeling, 114; role in product development, 111; and shipping, 114; and technology, 114–15; and testing, 111, 114

specification sheets ("spec" sheets), 109; Perry's example, *110*

Spotsylvania County (VA), 2; demographic information, *11–13*; retail sales history, *17*

SRI Consulting and Business Intelligence, 25. *See also* VALS survey

Stafford County (VA), 2; demographic information, *14–16*; retail sales history, *17*